Learning Along the Way

Learning Along the Way

**Professional Development
by and for Teachers**

Diane Sweeney

Literacy Specialist, Public Education & Business Coalition, Denver, Colorado

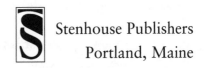

Stenhouse Publishers
Portland, Maine

Stenhouse Publishers
www.stenhouse.com

Library of Congress Cataloging-in-Publication Data
Sweeney, Diane.
    Learning along the way / Diane Sweeney.
    p. cm.
    Includes bibliographical references (p.) and index.
    ISBN 1-57110-343-0 (alk. paper)
    1. Early childhood education—United States. 2. Early childhood teachers—
United States. I. Title.
LB1139.25 .J35 2003
372.21—dc21   2002036572

Cover and interior photographs by the author

Manufactured in the United States of America on acid-free paper
09 08 07 06 05   9 8 7 6 5

This book is dedicated to my friends and colleagues at the Public Education & Business Coalition, an organization that never ceases to offer opportunities and challenges for learners of all ages.

Contents

Acknowledgments

I've never considered myself a lucky person. I haven't won a cent in Las Vegas and always get the busy signal during radio station giveaways. But when it comes to my experience as a teacher, I have been very lucky. I was lucky when I chose to teach at Harrington in Denver, Colorado. I was lucky when I became involved with the Public Education & Business Coalition (PEBC). And through all of that, I was lucky to have many mentors along the way. It was those mentors who helped me become a better teacher and staff developer, and it is those mentors whom I would like to thank for helping me write this book.

I've thought hard about whether I should be the one to tell this story. After all, I am one small part of a larger community. There are the staff developers from the PEBC such as Ellin Keene, Stephanie Harvey, Liz Stedem, Anne Goudvis, Lori Conrad, Marjory Ulm, Kristin Venable, and Chryse Hutchins, who developed this body of work over the past twenty years. How could I possibly share a professional development model that they created? There are the teachers who taught me how adults learn. Can I possibly speak for them?

After much consideration, I decided that this was a story that had to be told and that maybe I was the one to tell it. After all, I experienced the work firsthand, as a classroom teacher and instructional coach. I was the lucky one on the receiving end.

I'd like to thank Mariah Dickson, former director of PEBC Staff Development. Mariah painstakingly edited each word in this book and helped me figure out how to tell this story. Although I doubted my ability to actually write a book, Mariah never did.

My editors Philippa Stratton and Brenda Powers at Stenhouse Publishers trusted me and provided the feedback I needed to make it what it is today.

Barbara Volpe, the executive director of the PEBC, generously provided me with uninterrupted writing time and encouraged me every step of the way.

Rosann Ward, associate director at the PEBC, enthusiastically read my drafts and helped me polish them before publication. She told me that she would treat me like any other writer, which I appreciate more than she'll ever know.

Judy Hendricks, who has been dubbed "Queen of Everything" by the PEBC staff development team, holds everything together, while also serving as a surrogate mom and dear friend.

Also from the PEBC, Steph Harvey encouraged me to "just write the book." Chryse Hutchins has taught me a lot about teaching adults. And, of course, Ellin Keene developed the PEBC model of professional development that has shown permanence across time.

I was also lucky to find many friends and mentors while teaching at Harrington. Carole Quinby has been a close friend and teammate since the day we were both hired. I have learned more from Carole than from any other teacher, and I still hold on to the dream that some day I may teach with the same talent and grace that she possesses.

Rarely does someone get as lucky as I did when choosing a principal. At my interview, I was drawn in by Sally Edwards's charisma and energy, and that feeling has never passed even ten years later.

Marjory Ulm helped me switch from being a classroom teacher to taking on the new role of instructional coach. She was a mentor to both my literacy instruction and my work with adults.

Other teachers at Harrington helped me hone my ability as a staff developer. They were patient and taught me so much. They are Susan Levy, Christina Jensen, Amy Remmers, Keith Garvert, Lori Van Note, Lisi Quinby, Lesley Bowman, Irene Ribera, and many others.

I must not forget the most important people at Harrington—the children, who put a smile on my face and tears in my eyes on a daily basis.

I have also been lucky when it comes to receiving the unending support of my family. My parents pushed me to work hard and continue learning. My mom taught me to love books, and my dad always reminded me that education is of the highest importance.

And of course there's Dan, my wonderful husband, who didn't flinch when I came home one afternoon and told him I wanted to put off having babies to write a book. It was worth it, and around the time this book comes into the world, our first child will as well. It's been an exciting adventure that I truly couldn't have taken without him.

Suddenly those radio station giveaways don't seem so important. I am lucky.

Chapter 1

Principles of Professional Development

*It is virtually impossible to create and
sustain over time conditions for
productive learning for students when
they do not exist for teachers.*

—Seymour Sarason

The school parking lot fills a few minutes before 8 A.M. Lunches are stashed in the fridge and we head to our weekly professional development meeting. Teachers, classroom assistants, administrators, and the math and literacy coaches converge on the first-grade classroom where today's meeting will be held. Child-size chairs and desks fill the classroom, and an easel sits in the corner next to a small table draped with a colorful tablecloth and stacked with markers, a tape recorder, and a lamp radiating soft light. Beautiful picture books line the ledge beneath the chalkboard, and the walls are papered with writing, art projects, and other student work. Tables are grouped so children can work together, and atop each one sits brightly colored plastic bins of books and folders. It is clear that this is a classroom designed for children's learning. But for now, Christina's classroom will be home to teacher learning. For this hour, Starbucks mugs and half-eaten bagels rest next to the bins of children's books. For this hour our staff will come together to learn how to become better teachers of writing.

Writer's workshop is used throughout the school, and even with years of experience, many of us still struggle with both the organization of writing time and elevating the quality of student writing. With this in mind, a few teachers volunteered to share how they use writer's notebooks with their students. In the weeks before the meeting, every teacher was given a copy of Ralph Fletcher's *A*

Writer's Notebook: Unlocking the Writer Within You (1996), and today it will be a launching point for discussion. We begin with a general overview and description of writer's notebooks, and then, in the interest of giving everyone a chance to join the discussion, we break into small groups to talk about Fletcher's ideas.

As a literacy coach, I facilitate a discussion among three other teachers and begin with, "I'm thinking that using writer's notebooks is more true to the way writers really write."

"I think you're right," says Sue, "but I just don't know how to use writer's notebooks with kids. I feel like my writer's workshop is going well, and I'm not sure I want to add a whole new process."

Christina agrees. "With my first graders, I wonder how sophisticated they can get with something like a writer's notebook," she says. "I feel like I just got them used to the structure of writer's workshop, and switching scares me."

Paul asks, "Yeah, but is there any aspect of writer's workshop that isn't going well? Like something that you could change to help to make the kids' writing even better than it already is?"

Sue doesn't take long to answer that question. "You know, the revising process can be tough," she says. "All of my kids are at a different stage and I can't always spend the time I need to with them. I feel like I could use three more teachers in the room to make it manageable."

I wonder aloud if maybe writer's notebooks wouldn't help students in the revising process, because their ideas would be more developed before they even craft a piece of writing. We ponder that question along with many others and after awhile realize we have run out of time. I suggest that as their instructional coach, I would be happy to support anyone interested in trying writer's notebooks. Paul jumps at the offer: "Can we meet today after school? I'd love to get this going in my classroom," he says.

"I'll be there," I say as we scramble to throw away our coffee cups and push in our chairs. We know we just scratched the surface with today's discussion, but we will continue next week. Now it's time to begin our day with students.

Defining Learner-Centered Professional Development

In my first year teaching, the only professional development I received was an occasional inservice provided by the district. Usually these inservices failed to address whatever I was facing with my own students, and as a new teacher in a tough school, I needed much more.

The planners of these inservices usually did not understand that there is more to adult learning than an "expert" at an overhead projector with a vis-á-vis overhead marker at the ready. They didn't consider the learners in the darkened auditorium. Just as good teaching must meet diverse needs in a classroom, effective professional development must meet the individual needs of teachers. We know learning takes time; it isn't neat and tidy. So why do we believe it should be that way for teachers? Susan Loucks-Horsley writes, "[T]o be successful, professional development must be seen as a process, not an event" (1987). We would never base student learning upon a single experience, claiming, "I will teach all my students to read today with one, really great lesson." Learning is gradual and incremental, and one-shot inservices do not provide teachers with the necessary time or scaffolding to learn.

Adults learn in much the same way as children do. Pearson and Gallagher's gradual release of responsibility model (1983) demonstrates this for children, but it can be easily adapted to adult learners as well. In *Reading with Meaning: Teaching Comprehension in the Primary Grades* (2002), Debbie Miller writes, "If you think back to a time when you learned how to do something new, the gradual release of responsibility model comes into play." I agree with Debbie and wonder why professional development has failed for so long to consider the phases all learners move through toward new thinking. As educators, we are used to taking into account the diverse needs in a classroom of children, but the needs of adult learners are quickly forgotten. Adult learning is too often reduced to pulling together hundreds of teachers to listen to an expert pontificate on a given subject.

According to Pearson and Gallagher, children begin the learning process by watching a teacher model a strategy. Then, the student practices using the strategy with scaffolding, such as working in pairs, in small groups, or with a teacher. Finally, with time and practice, the student begins to use the strategy independently and in a variety of contexts.

Though the gradual release of responsibility model was designed to support reading instruction, a similar process occurs for any kind of learning. Consider the progression a golfer goes through when he learns to swing a club. The novice begins by watching an instructor demonstrate the swing. The instructor points out the specific techniques he uses, such as how he holds the club or where he positions his feet. Then the instructor helps the student get into the proper position to try to swing the club himself. Usually, on the first try, the novice either misses the ball entirely or makes a divot in the grass. The instructor continues to guide the student until he successfully hits the ball. The instructor gradually steps back and simply offers tips to improve the swing, and after awhile, the student is hitting on his own.

In contrast to the more traditional forms of teacher inservice, learner-centered professional development moves teachers through the same gradual release continuum beginning with modeling and demonstration. In this stage, the teacher observes exemplary instruction by participating in classroom observations, receiving coaching, watching professional development videos, and reading and discussing descriptions of effective instruction. The goal in this phase is to offer a visual picture of high-quality instruction. Just like a novice golfer learns by watching the instructor's swing, the modeling and demonstration phase allows teachers to observe exemplary instruction.

Next the teacher practices the approach that was previously modeled. In this phase, an instructional coach may teach alongside the teacher to offer feedback. Or teachers may participate in peer observations, meet in teams to discuss implementation of new teaching strategies, examine student work, or determine next steps in instruction. Without the guided practice phase, neither a golfer nor a teacher will improve, because feedback is essential for all learning.

When independence is reached, the teacher successfully integrates the new approach into his or her teaching. Depending on the teacher, independence may take several attempts in the earlier stages, because it depends on the teacher's knowledge base and the complexity of the new learning (see Figure 1.1).

One-shot inservices fail to give teachers the time and support they need to learn. In contrast, the gradual release continuum embeds the essential elements for successful and long-term learning. No wonder one-shot inservices usually feel like a waste of time. They usually are.

Harrington Elementary—A School That Fosters Adult Learning

I began my teaching career at Harrington, where I was a classroom teacher in the fourth and fifth grades. As I began my sixth year, the school offered me the chance to become an instructional coach. This gave me the opportunity to focus my attention on an area in which I had always been interested: adult learners. I spent the next two years as an instructional coach, and since then have been on staff with the Public Education & Business Coalition (PEBC), a nonprofit organization that provides professional development to teachers, principals, and instructional coaches across the Denver metropolitan area.

Harrington Elementary sits in a low-income neighborhood. The school building is new by most standards, having been completed in 1994 when the original building was deemed uninhabitable. Factories, warehouses, and railroad tracks occupy the area north of the school, and broken windows are evidence

Figure 1.1 Gradual Release of Responsibility Model for Adult Learning

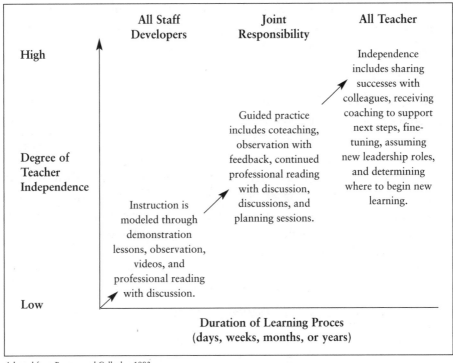

Adapted from Pearson and Gallagher 1983

that the buildings were abandoned many years ago. Across the street are tiny apartments housing extended families, and a nearby gas station sits on what has been dubbed one of the most dangerous street corners in Denver.

Somewhere between 500 and 550 students are at Harrington on any given day, many of whom come and go as their families struggle to find housing and employment. Approximately 76 percent are Hispanic, and 21 percent are African American. The other 3 percent are a combination of Anglo and Native American.

We will begin in 1994. I'd just barely survived my first year teaching a fourth- and fifth-grade combination classroom with thirty-three children who were all learning English. I spoke some Spanish but probably shouldn't have been deemed a "bilingual teacher." In many ways I was destined for failure. The teachers worked hard but weren't a team, literacy instruction wasn't articulated across grade levels, and student achievement was spotty. I chose to teach at Harrington because I wanted to work with low-income children, but many other teachers weren't at the school out of choice. They had been placed there because of a reduction in force at other schools in the district. There was an inconsistent delivery of instruction and a lack of collaboration among practically all the grade levels. It was then that Principal Sally Edwards decided to team up with the PEBC. With help from the PEBC, Harrington went through an eight-year transformation to become a committed community of learners.

Harrington is one example of a school that has defined how teacher learning affects student learning. The school has moved from being a fragmented and failing inner-city school to one that has developed a collaborative culture for both adults and children by honoring teachers' learning in relation to the gradual release continuum for learners. I believe this can happen at any school that chooses to offer learner-centered professional development.

This book is for the teachers, staff developers, and principals in schools who are working hard to figure out ways to build teacher learning into the school day. If you have ever dreamed of transforming your school into one with a shared vision, a shared knowledge base, and a shared approach to teaching, then you may find this story interesting.

Phases of Professional Development

The trend in school reform has moved toward schools purchasing "canned" professional development programs: programs that include lists and teacher scripts telling teachers exactly what to say and do. These programs are "grounded in educational research" and espouse the potential to "dramatically increase student achievement."

This is an oversimplified view of student and teacher learning. No two schools are alike, and one needs to take into account the complex nature of learning, for both students and teachers. Effective professional development is cyclical, ongoing, and can be divided into three phases: vision building, implementation, and sustainment.

Vision Building

The first year of professional development is dedicated to modeling high-quality literacy instruction. By providing models of good instruction a common vision and discourse evolves around teaching and learning. The term *vision building* commonly refers to organizational vision and is overused by both schools and businesses. On the other hand, the notion of vision is more concrete when it is grounded in instruction. In other words, staff developers help teachers define effective instruction and how it looks in the classroom. As the image becomes clear, teachers are more able to create a vision for their own instruction. Because modeling is the first stage on the gradual release continuum, professional development begins with observation, such as observation in lab classrooms or observation of a staff developer performing a demonstration lesson. Along with observation, vision building includes collaborative planning sessions, study groups, and book clubs.

When I was hired at Harrington, teachers were isolated and rarely questioned or shared what they were doing. Initial efforts to improve the school were structural, such as rearranging schedules, improving schoolwide discipline, and increasing parental involvement, and we rarely focused our efforts on teaching and learning. At the time, everyone taught writing differently, creating an environment in which the students were forced to adjust from one extreme to the other as they moved through the grade levels. Our isolationist perspectives changed when we embarked on a planning and vision-building process that spanned the next two years.

Sally understood that she needed to hire a content expert to support the staff as we struggled to define good writing instruction, so she brought in Marjory Ulm, a staff developer in writer's workshop. Marjory first modeled the writing process as we observed. Then we talked together about what we noticed and conferred about next steps. We discussed the kind of writing we expected our students to produce, we read books and articles about teaching writing, and we planned together. With time, a new language evolved. Prewriting, revising, editing, and publishing were common across all grade levels, and most important, students didn't have to adjust to a different writing curriculum year after year.

In one of our earliest conversations, Marjory asked me to define what I wanted for my students as writers. At the time, I couldn't answer that question because half the time, I had no idea what she was talking about: writing conferences, using a variety of genres, taking the writing to publication. None of this had been mentioned in my teacher education program. As a learner, I needed not only to learn the content and research but also to see the process modeled. Only then could I create my own understanding, be a part of the learning community, and contribute to the shared vision.

Implementation

Once a shared instructional vision is intact, the school is ready to move toward implementing it. Implementation includes more in-classroom coaching, observations in other classrooms or schools, and continued study of the research. Many of the professional development activities are the same in the planning and implementation phase, but the focus is different because there is now a shared understanding of why the changes are important, making this the time for guided practice. In this phase more than ever, staff developers need to understand the adults with whom they work. Otherwise, taking new learning into actual classroom practice will not necessarily be smooth sailing.

During the implementation phase at Harrington, Marjory began by emphasizing strategies such as conferring, generating topics, and managing a classroom of children all working on their own writing projects. As time went on, our focus became more sophisticated and we started to analyze student writing and compare our students' work with the state content standards. We learned about writing in a variety of genres, brainstormed a continuum of genres spanning grades K–5, and spent time learning about the text structures that good writers use.

Marjory spent a lot of time in my classroom and helping me during planning sessions. Sometimes I needed to run my ideas by her to make sure I was on the right track. She would give me the thumbs-up and I would carry out my plan. Other times, she suggested ways that my ideas could be improved; "What about trying . . ." or "Why not do . . ." were common phrases during those conversations. By that time, Marjory and I were getting to know each other, and I felt comfortable with her feedback.

The need to gear implementation toward the learner has become quite evident in my work as a staff developer. Every teacher with whom I have worked is an individual with unique experiences, and for staff development to succeed I have to be willing to support teachers as individuals. At the same time, I ask a lot from teachers, so they have to be able to trust my intentions. It takes trust to agree to be observed by your staff developer. It takes trust to admit that you need help. And it takes trust to have open conversations about what you are and are not willing to try with your students.

Several years ago, staff developer Colleen Buddy shared her perspectives on what it takes to succeed as a staff developer. At the time, I was a classroom teacher with no experience working with adults. I was struck not only by Colleen's humor and honesty, but by the messages she shared in her Staff Developer's Guiding Principles. Since then, I have read and reread her musings many times. Each rereading reminds me how to see the work through to implementation.

Colleen Buddy's Staff Developer's Guiding Principles
- *The Dick and Jane Principle:* Look! See! Take the time to observe the teacher with whom you are working so you will know how to move them forward in their learning. Remember, the gradual release continuum starts with the learner, not the staff developer.

- *The Spice Girls Principle:* Beware of fads. Stay grounded in the research and carefully evaluate new trends. Not everything out there is truly research based.
- *The Tortoise and the Hare Principle:* Pacing is an individual style issue. When it comes to pacing adult learning, be sensitive to the needs of the learner. Keep in mind the fact that the gradual release continuum isn't a straight line and that learning is recursive.
- *The Oprah Principle:* Relationships are the soul. Just like with kids, rapport is essential when working with adults. Take the time to get to know the teachers you work with both professionally and personally. It's not until a relationship is established that a teacher will be willing to take risks.
- *The Sistine Chapel Principle:* Masterpieces develop over time. Realize that adult learning takes time and that staff developers don't always have the benefit of seeing the product.
- *The Tomie dePaola Principle:* Stamp your heart on every page of your work. Just as with a classroom teacher, it is important to stay passionate about your work and let your own individual style come through.
- *The Great Debate Principle:* There is none. We all want literate lives for each other and ourselves. Steer clear from taking an "us versus them" stance. Maintain an open mind, and remember that we are all in it for the same reasons—the children.
- *The Leo the Late Bloomer Principle:* Each of us blooms in our own good time. Some teachers will take longer on the gradual release continuum. Keep modeling and offering feedback, and they will bloom in due time.
- *The Martha Stewart Principle:* Flowers, notes, and coffee count. Sometimes staff development is more like throwing a party, and these simple courtesies make the teachers you work with feel special and acknowledged.
- *The Monet Principle:* Observe the interplay of reality and reflection. Staff developers can provide a mirror for a teacher's practice. Through observation and feedback, the teacher is encouraged to reflect upon and consider his or her instruction.
- *The Dr. Seuss Principle:* Have fun! How else will teachers have the energy for such hard work?

Sustainment

If a faculty comes together as a learning community, the work will not only be sustained, but will continue to evolve. After three to five years, a school with an

----

established learning community is ready for independence, and the staff developer's role is to help the teachers sustain it on their own. When it comes to sustaining the work, every school faces its own unique challenges. Some may have high teacher turnover, so the learning community is reconfigured as the veteran teachers frantically try to help the new ones catch up. Other schools have to adapt to changes in curriculum and standards. The issues related to sustaining the work are school specific and dependent upon a principal and a staff of teachers who have vision and knowledge.

For a school to sustain a learning community, organizational changes may be called for. At Harrington, we reallocated positions to include two literacy coaches and one math coach to bolster our capacity for instructional coaching. We also reorganized the daily schedule to afford longer blocks of time and reconsidered our policy regarding classroom interruptions to make teaching time more sacred. In addition, we earmarked funds for future professional development, and teachers began looping across two grade levels so we could have more time with our students. Finally, we changed our traditional yearly calendar to one that was year-round, so we could offer intensive support to our struggling students during extended vacations. Each initiative was implemented gradually, and all were based on our newfound knowledge of educational research and student learning.

Together, we had learned about teaching and learning, and now we were more able to make collaborative decisions that supported our efforts. We were serious about making all that we had learned stick and were willing to make the changes that were essential to sustaining the work.

The research is clear when it comes to the importance of teacher learning. In her report *Doing What Matters Most: Investing in Quality Teaching* (1997), Linda Darling-Hammond cites teacher expertise as the most critical factor for improving America's schools: "Reforms, we have learned over and over again, are rendered effective or ineffective by the knowledge, skills, and commitments of those in schools. Without the know-how and buy-in, innovations do not succeed." In other words, professional development is important because good teaching is important. If you come at school change from the first line of defense, or the teacher, improvements will have a better chance at being sustained over time.

Effective professional development creates a learning environment in which teachers continue to improve their practice to better meet the needs of their students. By becoming a learning community, the teachers at Harrington were more prepared to address the challenges they faced in their classrooms. Teachers were expected to be learners and to work collaboratively, a responsibility that affected all members of the school community, most importantly the students.

Effective Professional Development Produces a Learning Community

In her book *In the Company of Children* (1996), Joanne Hindley stresses the importance of creating a community of learners where all children feel comfortable and can learn from each other. The same communities are critical when the learners are teachers. Just like our students, teachers need the opportunity to work with one another in a supportive environment. In order to learn, teachers need

- a collaborative environment where they feel safe and supported. In our classrooms, we strive for the very same sense of community. Sharing experiences and new ideas is a part of the school culture, and nobody feels isolated.
- leadership opportunities for all teachers regardless of their level of teaching experience. Knowledge is honored and leadership isn't left to a minority. Student ideas and successes are shared and celebrated so the children can learn from each other. The same goes for teachers.
- choice related to professional development. We offer an array of learning opportunities; however, within that choice lies a common vision and focus. Purposeful choice is essential to motivating students as well as teachers.
- feedback as an integral part of the school culture. Teachers cannot be left to carry on behind closed doors, but must be encouraged through observation and feedback. Teachers confer with students so students know whether they are on the right track or if they need more feedback about what to try next. Debriefing sessions with a staff developer yield the same outcome.
- access to resources. A professional library and classroom resources are available for the entire faculty. A well-supplied classroom helps teachers bring rich learning to their students. To learn, teachers need resources to draw upon just like kids.
- a clear set of shared goals and anticipated outcomes. Although learning among teachers is differentiated, the focus is clear and supported by all teachers. Students need to know why they are doing what they are doing, and the same goes for teachers.

Community isn't window dressing. It is much more. Hindley writes, "It is in building this community that we will lay the foundation for the year of academic learning but also for learning about people and the way we live in the world together. So we will 'work together' but equally as important, we will 'play together.'" Hindley's is a classroom that personifies learning based on collaboration, leadership, choice, feedback, access to resources, and a clear set of goals. This book will share how to create the same learning environment for teachers.

What About Resistant Learners?

Harrington's conversion to a professional development focus wasn't as easy as it sounds, and some of the faculty did everything they could to resist joining the learning community. Usually the reason wasn't that they had a bad attitude or were negative, though at the time it may have seemed that way. Teachers reject new knowledge and skills for a number of reasons, and our school was no different. Research shows that teachers reject new knowledge and skills when (Guskey and Huberman 1995)

- they are imposed (McLaughlin 1990);
- they are encountered in the context of multiple, contradictory, and overwhelming innovations (Werner 1988);
- most teachers, other than those selected for design teams, have been excluded from their development (Fullan 1991);
- they are packaged in off-site courses or one-shot workshops that are alien to the purposes and contexts of teachers' work (Little 1993);
- teachers experience them alone and are afraid of being criticized by colleagues or of being seen as elevating themselves on pedestals above them (Fullan and Hargreaves 1991).

A learning community mitigates these conditions. In a true learning community, teachers are trusted members of the process, and innovations are decided upon together and gradually build upon each other. If a school takes the time to build a learning community, teachers will be much less likely to resist change. In due time, a school will develop a solid vision, and teachers will trust themselves, each other, and the process they are moving through. Change becomes organic, building upon itself and evolving over time.

Practical Steps

Since learning communities are built upon an interdependent group of individuals with a set of common goals and a shared vision, no two learning communities are alike. Harrington evolved as a learning community through professional development based on the gradual release continuum, and each chapter of this book shares some examples of how it happened for us. Can another school replicate the steps to arrive at exactly the same outcome? Probably not. But each idea in this book can be used in any school setting to define a learning community of its own. From our experience, there are several questions to keep in mind.

Does your school draw from the existing knowledge pool? Sometimes schools hesitate to ask the more experienced teachers to step forward and share their knowledge. The most veteran teachers can be both honored and challenged by sharing what they know with others. Ask them to host an in-school lab, so other teachers can observe their teaching. Propose that they lead a study group with their favorite professional book or article. Using them as a resource will enable them to be learners as well and will tap into the knowledge that already exists in the school.

Do you consider professional development a complex endeavor? In professional development, it is tempting to generalize what the teachers should know and then start telling them what they are missing. Build upon what the teacher already knows, and more important, build upon their passions and interests. Motivation is just as important for teachers as it is for students, and learner-centered professional development can give teachers the energy they need to improve their instruction. Professional development can be a source of energy rather than an energy drain.

Do you encourage teacher reflection? Very few people can absorb all aspects of a learning experience and turn it into immediate action. We all need time to process information. When learning occurs over time and includes reflection, learners begin to adapt what they are learning to meet their own needs.

Do the teachers define their own learning goals? As a staff developer, it is important to begin with what the teacher is interested in learning. PEBC staff developers begin their work with questions such as, "What do you hope to get out of this experience?" or "What is keeping you up at night?" or "What can I help you with?" Teachers can usually pinpoint what they need from staff development, and that is where the staff developer can begin the work.

Do you listen to teachers? Effective professional development comes from the teachers. That means that as staff developers, we must *listen*. In conversations during professional development, teachers make revealing statements such as, "My students can't do that." On the surface this seems to be a simple comment, and it is easy to move on before tackling what it really means. There may be a thousand reasons why the teacher believes this is true, and it's the job of the staff developer to uncover the thinking behind the statement. Not until this understanding has been reached can a staff developer begin to move a teacher forward in his or her learning.

Is professional development considered scholarly? Are teachers familiar with a broad array of research and are their decisions based on sources such as university research, journal articles, the work of our colleagues, or findings from organizations such as the International Reading Association and the Rand Report? Learner-centered professional development depends upon teachers being willing to stay current so that they are not operating from hunches or trends but rather from research in the field of education.

Do you avoid the cute ideas? Learning is complex, and cute ideas can over-simplify the process. It's important for teachers to get concrete ideas out of professional development, and of course they need to feel that what they are learning applies directly to their workload. But at the same time, if we don't learn why we are doing things, we will never be empowered to make the decisions we will face in the future.

Do you spend time in faculty meetings only on matters that relate to student achievement? Faculty meetings are a rare opportunity for dialogue about student learning and professional development. With today's technology, communicating information is easier than ever. Schools rarely use e-mail as a way to communicate general information that takes time in faculty meetings. E-mail is a quick and easy way to share the latest news, resulting in more targeted professional development when the faculty comes together.

Do you base professional development on the teachers' self-interest? When teachers understand the research behind student learning, they are more able to determine the steps they need to move their students forward. When it comes to professional development, schools can define their own "mandates for learning" rather than depending on the district to furnish them.

A Final Thought

Hands-on learning is more common in today's classrooms, but is noticeably absent from professional development. Teachers build discussion and interest-based projects into the school day and are learning to accommodate their students' diverse needs and interests. Why can't the same be true for teacher learners? It is time to transfer our knowledge about student learning to teachers. If "sit and get" instruction isn't good enough for our students, then why is it good enough for teachers?

They say choosing a title is the most difficult part of writing a book. I started by keeping a running list of phrases I noticed myself using in my writing. *Learning Along the Way* started off my list. Even though I added several others, this one seemed to say the most because I intend to capture an array of examples of teacher learning: learning that is collaborative and ongoing, learning that spans time, learning that may be transformed or may transform a school environment, and teacher learning that encourages student learning.

At Harrington, professional development changed the way we viewed student learning. By learning together, we changed our point of view, changed our school community, and most important, changed our teaching. We were learning along the way.

Part 1

Modeling and Observation

Teacher educators often find themselves trying to capture high-quality instruction in words. Inservices, teacher education programs, and other training venues contain a lot of talk about good instruction but offer very few examples.

The gradual release continuum approaches the early stages of learning quite differently. Because every learner needs concrete models to visualize his or her own changes in practice, teacher learners are immersed in actual examples of exemplary instruction through professional reading and observations of instruction. Chapter 2 focuses on modeling high-quality instruction through study groups and teacher discussion. Chapter 3 offers an example of lab classrooms where instruction is modeled to participating teachers. Finally, Chapter 4 introduces instructional coaching as another means of modeling and demonstration.

Study Groups

It would be a great advantage to
some schoolmasters if they would
steal two hours a day from their pupils,
and give their own minds the benefit
of the robbery.

—J. F. Boyse

Carole and I sit at a library table loaded with piles of our favorite children's literature. Teachers filter in and collapse into the child-size chairs, wasting little time before sharing the day's triumphs and traumas. We are about to begin our first study group, and are eager to get started. Carole maneuvers the discussion by saying, "Thanks for taking the time to come to our first meeting. We hope that exploring poetry will benefit all of us personally and professionally."

As Carole speaks, I glance at the faces around the table. When we were planning the study group, we were aware of the possibility that no one would be interested in this type of professional development. I am encouraged when I count fourteen colleagues, including teachers from across the grade levels, the librarian, and the principal.

Predictably, the teachers in attendance represent the most involved teachers in the school. As is the case in many schools, Harrington has two distinct groups of teachers: those who thrive on professional development, and those who are more reticent to get involved. We are relieved to have a turnout, but wonder how to reach the rest of the teachers on our staff.

Then to our surprise, Marsha wanders in and joins us. Carole had mentioned the gathering to Marsha earlier in the day, but she hadn't planned to attend, and we are pleased that she has changed her mind. Even though she is an accomplished teacher, Marsha usually avoids professional conversations, opts out of professional learning opportunities, and seems to be most content teaching at the end of the hall with the door closed.

She pulls up a chair, carefully positioning herself behind the other members of the group. I encourage her to squeeze in with the rest of us, but she declines, and I decide not to push it because I am happy she decided to come in the first place.

We begin by sharing how we use poetry with our students. Cindy says, "I like to read my kids a poem without showing them the pictures. Then I hold up the picture and tell them to compare the picture in their mind with the picture in the book."

I add, "You can really teach the strategy of sensory images with almost any poem since poetry is so descriptive."

Marsha doesn't take long to get involved in the conversation and says, "I don't know why, but I'm not very comfortable teaching poetry." She begins to explain her feeling that poetry has a single correct interpretation. Her experiences as a student of poetry left her feeling as if everyone else understood the deeper meanings, whereas she struggled to find any meaning at all. Cindy, on the other hand, has always loved poetry and takes any opportunity she can to discuss it with friends and colleagues. Carole and I quickly realize that getting this group to reflect deeply on their ideas about poetry won't be as difficult as we anticipated.

The weeks pass, and our study group rolls along at a steady pace. Our discussions are dynamic and leave us thinking about poetry in new ways. On one of those thank-goodness-it's-finally-spring afternoons, Marsha clears her throat and announces that she wants to share a poem—the first she has ever written. The silence is immediate as she reaches into her bag and pulls out a neatly typed piece of paper. She reads, never lifting her eyes from the page, and then waits for a response from the group. We struggle for something to say. How do you come up with a quick and easy response to someone who has just risked so much? All we can do is sigh, ruminate on the lines within her stanzas, and ask her to read it again.

When she reads the last line for the second time, the group doesn't hold back. Cathy says, "You paint such a picture with your words."

Pat agrees: "I can really feel your energy." Someone brings up Marsha's earlier comment that there was one interpretation for a poem, and we all laugh about how far we have come.

After a few months, we realize that we are learning about more than just poetry. Marsha is learning to consider herself a writer and has begun to trust her colleagues. I have been introduced to the poetry of Langston Hughes, who still reigns as my all-time favorite poet. Teachers are bringing poetry to their students in new and creative ways. A shared vision and common language is being forged out of laughter, and shared ideas and passions have been stirred up that give us the energy to teach. It is a sacred and scholarly time.

Building Community by Making Our Teaching Public

Education is no longer an autonomous profession wrought with covert teaching. By offering a content-based study group, we made our teaching public. Our study group also served as a point of entry on the gradual release continuum. For teachers who may not have been ready to tackle poetry in their own classrooms, the reading and discussion that took place during our study group offered a glimpse at how others teach poetry. We enhanced our relationships by encouraging teachers to share with colleagues, we learned by exploring, and we took greater risks similar to those that we expect our students to take. Our poetry study group was a first step in determining a schoolwide instructional vision, a vision that depends on the following elements:

Discourse

Professional discourse is one of the more effective ways to create a common vision. Public service announcements encourage families to sit down together during mealtime to stay connected with one another. The same goes for a faculty. Unfortunately, few schools provide their teachers the opportunity for professional discourse. As schools struggle to invest in teacher growth, many are taking a "binder approach." The principal gives the teacher a binder with pages describing the latest program, assuming that implementation will be a breeze and that test scores will go up. The binder approach is actually counterproductive to the vision-building process, because many such programs are designed to be "teacher-proof." When teachers are handed a binder, they are given the message that the program is fully developed and will be successful in every classroom. This results in more covert teaching because programs of this kind are not flexible, leaving little to talk about. Study groups, on the other hand, provide ample opportunities for teacher input and discussion, because they are designed to be flexible and offer no predetermined outcomes.

Intimacy

Intimacy is a sense of connectedness between individuals. For learners to take risks, they have to feel that they can trust and be trusted. In the poetry study group, we learned that merely having conversations about one's ideas can be threatening. Marsha was probably thinking, "If I say something, everyone will know how little I actually know about poetry." Cindy may have thought, "I don't want to dominate the conversation and make everyone think I'm a know-it-all." All learners, whether big or small, have these inner conversations, and in an intimate learning community these individual differences aren't a barrier to learning, as long as each member of the group feels comfortable taking chances.

Discovery

Webster's defines the word *discovery* as "[t]o find by exploration." In a professional development environment based on discovery, the outcomes aren't apparent in the beginning. Instead, teachers engage in a process of exploration and discovery to come to some unknown conclusion. There are more questions than answers, and the group creates new understanding together. Making such discoveries motivates learners, and offering teachers the chance to be inspired by new discoveries is a fundamental part of study groups.

I've found that each study group I facilitate takes on a life of its own. Members of the group bring ideas, share resources, and help set the agenda. At Harrington, someone suggested we read Georgia Heard's *For the Good of the Earth and the Sun* (1989) along with articles from professional journals, so that's what we did.

Community

In *Life in a Crowded Place* (1992), Ralph Peterson suggests that learning is community based, and writes,

> It has to do with developing our expressive abilities and participating in everything that interests us, with being able to benefit from the insight and experience of others as we work at making the world take on meaning for ourselves, with living and learning in a place outfitted with opportunities to learn, a place where we can fumble and make mistakes without being scorned or laughed at. And it has to do with being responsible for our own learning. In short, it has to *mean* something to us.

Peterson is absolutely right when he says that learning has to mean something, and for a study group to mean something, it has to be voluntary and driven by the participants' interests.

Variations on a Theme

Since our first study group, many more have been formed in various shapes and sizes. The teachers who were noticeably absent the first time have gradually become more involved.

Study groups are created to support teachers new to the profession or new to the school. The latest best-selling professional book may trigger a teacher to start a study group. When my fellow staff developers at the Public Education & Business Coalition, Stephanie Harvey and Anne Goudvis, published *Strategies That Work: Teaching Comprehension to Enhance Understanding* (2000), the staff decided to venture away from the school and make the study group a festive occasion by meeting at a local brewery on a Friday afternoon. Sally told me, "You know, Diane, I didn't think many people would come, with their family obligations and after such a long week." She was proven wrong when twenty-two of the thirty-three teachers showed up ready to participate.

We also enjoy discussing adult literature in a teacher book club. Every month, Carole invites interested staff members to her house for dinner and a book discussion. With a decidedly less educational tone, the group enjoys reading the latest adult literature, sharing a few glasses of wine, and laughing a lot.

Study groups come in all shapes and sizes and meet different kinds of needs. At Harrington, our study groups have been most effective when they are needs based, and are rarely successful when a single person defines the goals for the group.

Practical Steps

What should you consider when planning a study group?

We have found that study groups are most effective when they

1. are voluntary;
2. involve participants in the decision-making process regarding the content, facilitation, and focus;
3. reflect regularly on whether the time spent has been productive;
4. include rituals and celebrations;
5. determine norms and procedures as a group;
6. spend little time discussing unpopular district or school policies;
7. consider the study group a time for sharing and discovery;
8. avoid assuming that certain participants are experts; and

9. include a diverse set of staff members, such as teachers, the principal, the librarian, special education teachers, and other members of the school community.

Considerations for Study Group Facilitation

Teachers are usually comfortable setting norms for children, but much less comfortable doing so for themselves. Just like in the classroom, the community functions more smoothly if participants are clear about how the study group will function, so take the time to create a well-understood set of norms at your first meeting, reviewing them as necessary. When setting norms in your study group, consider the following:

1. Who will facilitate the meetings? Will the facilitator rotate between participants?
2. How will the group honor differing opinions?
3. Who will select the focus and content of the study group? Will the focus change, or stay the same?
4. How will the group be sensitive to the time constraints of others? How punctual do participants expect to be? Should the group plan to get started at the designated time, or wait for stragglers? What is the most convenient time for everyone involved? What about running over the allotted time?
5. Will the discussions be predictable, or does the group want to "go with the flow"? Some adults like a very structured agenda, whereas others prefer a conversational style.
6. Will participants be expected to read between meetings? What happens if members fail to keep up with their reading?
7. Does the group need reminders about upcoming meetings? If so, who will be responsible?
8. How will the group assess progress?

What should we talk about in our study group? The options are endless when it comes to organizing study groups. Topics might include

1. Reading adult literature to assess one's own methods of reading comprehension. Adult readers take their processes for comprehending text for granted. Read challenging literature with your colleagues while keeping in mind your use of the comprehension strategies. Either focus on one strategy at a time, or think about them holistically. Then share your thinking

and consider how it relates to your students. (For a list of great adult literature, see Appendix 2.)

2. Analyzing elements of high-quality writing in adult or children's literature. Examine the characteristics of a particular genre of writing as a way of determining the elements that should be taught to students.

3. Sharing original writing by children or adults. Discuss issues such as teacher expectations for student proficiency and the rigor of the school's writing program.

4. Reading and responding to professional literature. When considering the needs of the school, think about choosing professional readings that will complement teacher learning.

5. Considering standards-based instruction as it applies to the school setting. Every school has a unique set of needs that can be considered before implementing a standards-based program. Share personal views and concerns before implementing a reform.

6. Exploring specific genres such as poetry, historical fiction, or expository text. Students should be exposed to multiple genres, and study groups designed to motivate teachers to explore a variety of genres will raise the number that they offer their students.

7. Sharing key learnings. Use study groups as a venue for teachers to share what they have learned at conferences, institutes, and workshops with the rest of the faculty.

8. Jigsawing articles or short pieces. Sometimes it isn't appropriate to read an entire book or article in a study group. Occasionally, use the jigsaw approach, where the text is divided into sections for individual teachers to read and share with the rest of the group.

9. Analyzing data to solve a dilemma or challenge that the school is facing. When a school struggles with a particular issue, data collection can be a more objective way to seek a solution.

10. Reviewing and discussing educational videos. Publishers produce high-quality videos designed for staff development purposes. They can be used in study groups as a starting point for discussion.

Videos and Study Groups

Some schools do not have the resources to observe in other classrooms, and because modeling is the first phase on the gradual release continuum, videos can play a valuable role in study groups. Videos are useful tools to paint a picture of effective instruction without the teachers ever leaving the school site. Educational publishers are producing videos to accompany many of their books

and materials. For example, when I worked with a group of teachers on conferring with students, I used Joanne Hindley's video set titled *Inside Reading and
Writing Workshops* (1998) that accompanies her book *In the Company of
Children* (1996). When I worked with teachers on reading comprehension, the
video set *Strategy Instruction in Action* that accompanies Stephanie Harvey and
Anne Goudvis's *Strategies That Work* (2000) was very helpful. Videos take
teacher learning further. Instead of merely describing what I mean by "effective
instruction" I am able to show them. (For a list of videos, see Appendix 1.)

Other Ideas for Study Groups

Time is a precious resource for any school. When organizing a study group, consider the following ideas to help make them time-efficient and practical:

1. meet in grade-level teams, vertical teams, or by specialty;
2. include teachers from a neighboring school;
3. use faculty meeting time for study groups;
4. use a study group as a means of initiating teacher research projects;
5. observe a colleague as he or she tries a new teaching strategy with children
   during a study group.

A Final Thought

Educators work hard to create learning opportunities for their students and
rarely get to participate in it themselves, in effect keeping learning at a distance.
Study groups fit within both the contexts of the gradual release of responsibility
continuum and the learning community. For that reason, they are a thoughtful
way to transfer the focus away from inservice and toward teacher learning, a
paradigm shift in today's schools where impersonal and decontextualized inservice has been the norm for so long.

Chapter 3

Understanding Through Observation

Who dares to teach, must never
cease to learn.

—John Cotton Dana

Six teachers walk into Carole's fourth-grade classroom and gaze around. Someone asks, "Where do you put the kids?" It's our first of four days in Carole's lab, and the visiting teachers quickly realize they have been given the chance to observe an exemplary teacher for four full days, a rare opportunity in the teaching profession. In only a few minutes they are already awestruck.

The classroom overflows with books, with the total hovering around 8,000. The walls are lined with homemade, store-bought, and hand-me-down bookshelves. In addition to the books on shelves, baskets of titles by favorite authors rest in the last bits of available space. Once a younger student wandered into Carole's classroom, looked around, and asked in a quiet voice, "Is this the library?"

Carole laughed and remarked, "That is the biggest compliment anyone could pay me."

I explain to the lab participants that we will spend the mornings observing Carole's literacy instruction and the afternoons debriefing. As Carole's lab facilitator, my job will be to help the teachers connect what they see to their own instruction. I will do this by leading a discussion beforehand and a debriefing session afterward, supplying professional articles and book suggestions, and serving as a buffer between Carole and her visitors so she can carry on with her teaching as if we aren't there. This year our group consists of three teachers from a neighboring school, two interns at the Rocky Mountain School of Expeditionary Learning, and a first-year teacher from Harrington.

On our first visit, I gather the teachers and begin by asking what they hope to get out of the time they will spend observing Carole. Yves doesn't hesitate: "I want to see a group of disadvantaged kids love reading like I do."

Brenda adds, "I hope to learn how to engage kids because, to be honest, I am really struggling with management in my classroom."

Jessica is working on her definition of constructivism. Because Mira is an art teacher, she wants to know how what she will see in Carole's classroom will inform her art instruction. Richelle and Darlene would like to give their fourth graders more choices but aren't sure how to manage it all. I think about Carole's classroom and reply, "You are all in the right place."

Establishing Observation Norms

In my early days as a lab facilitator, I assumed teachers knew what to expect from observing in labs. I failed to realize that many teachers have spent very little time observing in other classrooms, and soon learned that the better job I did establishing norms in the beginning, the quicker the group became a learning community. Now I set aside time to discuss the observation norms before a lab ever begins. That way the teachers get the most they can out of the experience, and I've staved off potential problems. (For more on observation guidelines, see "Practical Steps.")

Not until we have discussed the observation guidelines is our lab group ready to get started. We glance at the clock and realize that it is nearing 8:50 and that the bell will ring any minute. We rush to stash our coats and backpacks and to get our notebooks ready as Carole's students quietly file in and head straight for their seats. Each child immediately chooses a book from the box sitting at the center of his or her table and begins reading.

Carole starts the day by pulling aside a small group for a reading conference. Rachel, Brianna, and Jesus have been reading Cynthia Rylant's short story "The Pet" (1985). Carole leads off by asking, "Did you have any trouble spots when you read the story?"

Rachel says, "A little bit," and tells the group about the parts of the story that left her confused.

Carole says, "If you are interested in using sticky notes, help yourself." She points to the small container in the center of the table that is filled with hot pink Post-it pads. Then she adds, "What do you think you should mark?"

Brianna says, "The important parts."

Jesus adds, "The places where we got stuck."

Carole asks, "What's your code going to be?"

The kids suggest codes to write on their sticky notes. She hands them a good supply and sends them back to their seats to continue.

As Carole talks with her students, the teachers huddle around, recording every word. They want to know what she writes in her notebook and peer over her shoulder to get a better look.

Several minutes later, a student rings a brass bell and everyone gathers on the carpet in the front of the room. Carole opens a book and starts reading. Both the children and teachers hang on every word. The students regularly raise their hands to chime in their ideas and connections to the story, and the teachers record it all in their notebooks. We are learning together, adults and children.

The morning continues with more examples of thoughtful instruction. We finish by observing the first day of book clubs and a bit of geography. I glance around the room at the other teachers and can tell they are ready to find out how Carole does it all. The students are dismissed to lunch, and we head to a nearby Mexican restaurant for our debriefing session.

During any lab debriefing session, participants are eager to ask the lab teacher questions about her practice. It's the facilitator's job to make sure the discussion answers the participants' logistical questions such as, "What do you keep in the boxes on student desks?" or "When do you teach math and science?" But I also need to make sure teachers learn how to reflect on the lab teacher's purposes and then relate it to their own practice. In the debriefing, I spend a lot of time listening and taking notes. That way, I begin to understand the participants' needs. Then I chime in with probing questions or suggestions, and I always ask the participants to leave with something specific they plan to take back to their own classrooms.

In today's debriefing session, Brenda says, "I noticed that each child feels important in Carole's class. They are all engaged, and everyone is allowed to have an opinion. There is no right or wrong answer."

I make a note that after one day she is beginning to figure out the connection between honoring individual ideas and authentic engagement. Then I ask her, "What do you think that means for your instruction? Can you forge that link between acknowledgment and engagement?"

Brenda thinks for a minute and replies, "I have been struggling with classroom management and I get frustrated when my students have a negative attitude. Maybe I need to think about the messages I'm sending them."

The conversation turns to Carole's methods for staying on top of her individualized reading instruction and Yves asks, "How on earth do you keep it all organized?"

Carole is ready for this question since someone always asks it on the first day of lab. She explains how she organizes her reading block and tells the group how it works: "I start by modeling the tasks with the whole class. Then, each time we do a book study, the class decides which tasks they would like to do. For example when we were reading about the Revolutionary War, the students chose to do a Venn diagram to compare King George III with George Washington. We are careful to balance reading comprehension, vocabulary, and fluency." The rest of the first day is spent discussing the ins and outs of managing reading instruction.

Our discussion bounces from one topic to another. The chips and salsa have been cleared, we are on our third refill of soda, and we scribble in the notebooks still sitting in front of each of us. Before we break for the day, I ask everyone to share something they plan to work on between now and our next lab visit. I carefully note their ideas and will start our next discussion by asking how it went.

Observing Across Days

Observing across days is like peeling off the layers of an onion. On the first day, the teachers are usually interested in how the classroom is organized. After they have asked the organizational questions, they begin to observe instruction more keenly. The questions inevitably become more multifaceted and the teachers begin to see past the surface to gain new perspectives on high-quality teaching.

As the days pass, our group begins to see the threads that are woven through Carole's literacy instruction. They gain insight into how she offers choice to her students by observing the many options she gives them on different days, in various subjects, and in different ways. They learn more about her rapport with students and begin to understand why they are such eager learners. They see how she handles the challenges, such as a new student who arrives from Mexico in April and doesn't know the name of his hometown. Observing for one day would give the teachers a small taste, but not enough to carry them forward.

Many schools and districts have broken literacy instruction into bits and pieces and have not addressed the big picture, and one of the challenges of facilitating a lab is helping teachers understand the complexity of good literacy instruction. Labs acknowledge the fact that meeting the literacy needs of an entire classroom of children isn't easy and that teachers can get where they need to go only by considering the big questions. One day is not enough time to understand how a teacher moves her students forward as learners. Some teachers resist our requirement that they attend labs over several days, and ask to see a variety of teachers rather than just one. We hold our ground, though, because we know that questions about literacy cannot be answered with a few new activities.

Facilitating Changes in Practice

A prominent feature of the lab model is the opportunity for reflection and self-assessment. Lab classrooms offer varied examples of high-quality instruction, and participants are supported as they work to improve their instruction. The minute participants walk into a lab classroom, they are encouraged to think reflectively about what they see. In Carole's lab the first reaction is always the literate environment she has created for her students. Lab participants wonder how they could ever attain a classroom library anywhere near the depth of Carole's. I never want the lab participants to leave believing they can never offer the same array of books, so I make sure to have Carole explain how she has accumulated such an extensive collection. Once they get past the classroom environment, they wonder how she creates such an unquenchable thirst for learning. These kids take their learning seriously. This one is a bit more difficult to explain. Carole articulates her beliefs about learning and says that choice is one of the ways she motivates her students. As her facilitator, I fill in the blanks.

Inevitably, teachers compare their classroom with Carole's, which can be overwhelming and sometimes leaves them thinking they will never measure up. When the discussion moves in this direction, I encourage Carole to share how she has become the teacher she is today. I also suggest that participants avoid trying to replicate everything they see but instead choose one thing to bring back to their classrooms. This process of self-assessment encourages teachers to go back and improve their own instruction.

Rebecca was a second-year teacher who participated in a four-day lab. In a discussion at the end of her experience, she reflected on how being in a lab changed her teaching:

> The labs were relevant. I could take what I saw back to my classroom since I had seen it work. At first, I thought I had to do it all at once. Then in the debriefing, the facilitator said to pick one thing to start with, so I began by rearranging the physical aspects of my room. I changed the schedule and moved the desks, so my students could have conversations. Later, I started turning over more responsibility to my students. Now, teaching reading feels like a natural thing, a part of life.

Reflecting on her own teaching as she observed in the lab classroom, Rebecca began to assess her practices. She then made changes based on what she had seen.

It is now mid-December, and our group is meeting for the third time. When we gather before the students arrive, I ask the group, "What have you tried since the last time we met?"

Darlene says, "I have been trying to confer with my students. I have them come to me and we talk about what they are reading."

Brenda says, "I started book clubs, and they are going pretty well so far. I am just having trouble convincing my students to reread."

Richelle completely rearranged her classroom and began giving her students more opportunity to make choices based on their interests. Today she wants to observe the way Carole asks her students questions.

We spend the next morning observing and look forward to the ensuing conversation. In our debriefing session, Jessica sums it up when she says, "I've learned a lot of management strategies, but more than that, I've learned that it's really okay to teach kids that they should be loving reading. I don't want them to view reading as a tool—I want it to be a part of their lives."

How Can I Create a Lab Network in My School or District?

In 1991, staff developers Stephanie Harvey and Liz Stedem were heading back to Denver after spending a few days with staff developers at Teachers' College in New York. Part of their visit included an observation day in Judy Davis's classroom, where Steph and Liz were struck not only by the quality of the teaching, but also by the effect of the observation itself. Sitting in Judy's classroom gave a complete picture of high-quality literacy instruction. Steph and Liz were able to experience the literate community Judy had established and to see how the students learned in their own setting. They quickly realized that observing an exemplary teacher produces an authentic opportunity to learn within the context of a real classroom. While flying home, they began planning how they would offer this experience to teachers in Denver.

They started by considering a handful of potential lab classrooms. Lab teachers had to be reflective, know and exemplify the educational research, and be able to share their knowledge with others. Furthermore, their classrooms had to be magical places—rooms filled with books and students who lived literate lives. They chose Debbie Miller, Kathy Haller, and Bruce Morgan.

Next Steph and Liz considered who would facilitate the labs. The facilitator also had to be familiar with the educational research, understand how to stimulate adult learning, and know the lab teacher. Liz, Steph, and Ellin Keene became the first lab facilitators.

When Steph and Liz shared their groundbreaking idea with the three lab teachers, they were, as Debbie puts it, "excited and sick at the same time." For the first time, they would be opening up their classrooms to strangers, and their instruction would be analyzed and openly discussed. They knew that what they offered had to be good. Debbie decided to offer a look at reader's workshop in her first-grade classroom. Kathy taught kindergarten and her focus was on emergent writing. In his upper-grade classroom, Bruce's lab explored writing workshop with the teachers writing together and then discussing what their own writing taught them about teaching children to write. That was more than ten years ago, and now the lab network they created has grown to fifteen labs ranging from kindergarten to high school.

Any school, district, or professional development organization can establish its own lab network. After the Boulder Valley School District had been involved in professional development for several years, staff developers Anne Goudvis and Bobbie Benson helped the district create its own lab network. Because the district had taken the time to improve upon the excellence of the teachers, the natural progression was to share what had been learned with other teachers in the district.

The first step was to create a list of a few of Boulder's promising teachers. Once the teachers were selected, Anne and Bobbie carefully planned how they would support them. They decided that the first step would be to send them to observe in other classrooms so they could anticipate what to expect from being a lab teacher. Anne and Bobbie also helped the lab teachers with their plans because the teachers were worried about having something to offer their classroom visitors. At last, they opened their classrooms to observers. Now Boulder Valley hosts six labs focusing on reading comprehension, bilingual literacy instruction, and instruction in the library setting. Their labs are open to anyone in the district and take place over four days.

Practical Steps

The best way to begin a lab network is to start small. Choose just a few extraordinary teachers and build from there, because they are what make a lab successful. The following criteria can be useful when selecting lab teachers. Lab teachers

- have participated in extensive professional development;
- have observed in other classrooms;
- are thoughtful about teaching and learning;
- demonstrate research-based teaching in a real context;
- have the confidence to host visitors in their classrooms;
- are capable of discussing the purposes behind what they do with their students;

- understand, articulate, and exemplify educational research;
- are authentic readers and writers;
- set a positive tone in the classroom;
- are passionate about teaching;
- demonstrate a rigorous approach to learning;
- are articulate about their purposes and choices as teachers;
- are reflective;
- view themselves as learners;
- continue to evolve as teachers.

Lab Facilitation

Good facilitation is also vital to ensure that labs are a productive experience. It can be tempting to go as far as setting up an opportunity for teachers to observe each other without arranging facilitation, but without good facilitation, labs lose the power to engage teachers in thoughtful discussion about their practice. The most effective lab facilitators

- understand best practice;
- are familiar with the teaching style of the lab teacher;
- can be firm when setting expectations for participants;
- ask open-ended questions;
- honor each participant's perspective;
- recognize and can name aspects of high-quality teaching;
- can suggest ways for participants to begin implementing what they observe;
- are effective note-takers;
- move conversations from the surface observations to the deeper ideas and purposes behind them;
- make connections across visits;
- model the behavior of a good observer;
- ask participants to connect and respond to what they observe;
- empathize with the demands on participants while helping them move forward.

Observation Guidelines

My friend and colleague Chryse Hutchins taught me how to establish norms before ever beginning a lab observation. The following list comes from her years of experience as a lab facilitator and has proven to be a useful way to set the tone with any lab group.

Leave no trace. Classrooms are organic and full of underlying relationships and messages. Take care not to affect the community in any way. That means that when we have the desire to help a student spell a word, tie a shoe, or even just remark about what a nice job he is doing, we must refrain.

Silence is golden. The process of observing should stir up new ideas and questions, but wait until the debriefing to start the discussion. It can be challenging to bite our tongues because it might feel as if we are missing the opportunity to ask an important question. This is the reason why debriefing sessions are vital. If an opportunity to talk together isn't scheduled, teachers will feel compelled to debrief during the observation.

Honor the lab teacher. Acknowledge the fact that lab teachers are human and have good and bad days. As a lab group, we are not there to seek faults in the lab teacher, but to learn from him or her.

Take notes. Lab participants are expected to take notes. Some lab facilitators create handmade notebooks for the teachers in their labs, sending the message that note taking is an important part of the experience. They also go as far as to recommend methods for note taking and share their own observation notebooks as a model. (For more on this see "Note Taking.")

Observe across visits and expect gradual change of practice. The most effective labs are from four to six days long. Suggest that participants observe for something specific; otherwise they may feel overwhelmed by all they see. At the beginning of each visit, I ask, "What are you planning to look for today?" By knowing what they are hoping to learn, it is easier for me to focus the observation. Sometimes, one focus continues across visits and I take notes specifically on that topic. Then I regularly come back to my notes to be sure we have addressed each individual's issues. When teachers are encouraged to think about small ways they can evolve in their teaching, the process of bringing new ideas back to the classroom is less daunting.

Get involved in the discussion. Debriefing sessions are not a time to be shy, and having a safe community is important for the less confident members of the group. Lab participants should know that this is their chance to get their questions answered, no matter how big or small.

Do your homework. Labs involve professional reading. Participants need to know that they will be expected to keep up with the reading, because the discussion breaks down quickly when a few members of the group don't follow through. It needn't always be the lab facilitator's job to lead the discussion. Think about inviting group members to trade off taking the role as facilitator.

It's not our turn to teach. One thing is for sure: teachers relish teaching. When participating in a lab, it can be challenging to step out of the teacher role. The most important thing to think about during a lab observation is what the lab teacher is doing. We remind lab participants to stay close to the lab teacher and to listen in on all the conversations she has with students. When the time comes for students to do independent work, we encourage the teachers to follow the lab teacher to see what she does, and resist the urge to intervene with a student.

Note Taking

I have visited Carole's classroom hundreds of times by now, and I always find something new to record. Maybe it is the title of a book she used that I haven't seen. Or perhaps a reading conference I listened to that was interesting. On every visit, I write pages of notes both for my benefit and to model the importance of note taking to the other lab participants.

I tell participants up front that the better the notes they take, the richer the debriefing session will be in the afternoon. Nobody can hold an entire observation in their memory, so I make it clear that I expect to see lots of writing during the observation.

When teaching lab participants my expectations around note taking I show them my observation notebook. I use two-column notes, writing what the lab teacher does on the right side and my questions, ideas, or reflections on the left. Then in the debriefing session, I can skim down the left side to come up with ideas I'd like to bring up with the group. I usually give each lab participant his or her own composition book that is covered in bright, colorful fabric. Then they know I'm serious.

I'm also sure to bring my notes from the previous visits so I can refer to what was discussed on earlier days. For example, I may ask Brenda, "How is your classroom management going now that you've been thinking about ways to honor your students?" Without my notes I'd never remember the discussion we had months earlier. Sometimes, I take notes specific to a participant's question. For example, when someone asked if Carole used a guided reading approach, I jotted down all the examples I saw of guided reading on that given morning. When we debriefed, I shared these with the group. Both the facilitator's and the participants' note taking is a tool to move the conversation to a deeper level (see Figure 3.1).

Figure 3.1 Pages from My Observation Notebook

Carole Quinby's Lab - Day 2

I ask lab participants - what do you
    plan to observe for today?
Sergio: How do you teach the reading comprehension
        strategies to new kids? Today he wants
        to observe a new student from Mexico
        named Jaime.
Mary Ann: What do you do with children
        who are struggling readers?
Jeanie: How do you incorporate reading
        comprehension into daily reading?
Darlene: How do you manage behavior? Today
        she plans to observe James, a child
        who struggles with behavior.
Stacy: How do you encourage independence
        and choice among students?

Observation Notes - Day 2

It looks like   Carole begins the day with
every day starts   daily math. Children head
like this. The   right to their seats and
routine helps   begin working the problem.
with management.
                     Janice struggles and Carole
                     spends a few minutes helping
                     her.

Jamie just   Jamie finishes the math and
arrived from   pulls out a Spanish book
Mexico. He   about cars. He seems to be
only speaks   authentically engaged in the
Spanish and   book.
has had
little schooling.

He likes the
book and probably
likes racecars.

A typical lab day includes a conversation before school, the observation itself, and a debriefing session afterward. Here's our schedule from Carole's lab:

8:00–8:50	Meet in the classroom. The first meeting is the time to go over the observation norms. If it isn't the first day, we discuss what we have tried since last time and share what we hope to watch for today.
8:50–11:30	Observe instruction.
11:30–3:00	Debriefing is a combination of questions for Carole, discussion of the readings, and sharing ideas and next steps.

A Final Thought

Isolation is a regular part of school life. Teachers feel isolated within their classroom, and schools feel isolated within the greater community.

Four years ago, when groups of teachers began arriving at Harrington to observe in Carole's classroom, the other teachers in the school noticed. They wanted to know why the visitors were there and what they were missing out on. This became a catalyst for change, and the fact that the school had made the transition from receiving professional development to being a place that offered it wasn't lost on the teachers. Pride can be hard to come by in a school that struggles with test scores and the day-to-day realities of poverty, and running into visitors in the hallway became an instant source of pride.

Sally quickly recognized the benefits that labs could have for her teachers. In a school with high teacher and student turnover, she covets professional development opportunities that help her keep her teachers renewed and ready to move their students forward. She has made labs available to many of her teachers with the only requirement being that they share what they learn with the rest of the staff. That way, ideas are cross-pollinated. More important, a common language has been forged, teachers are held accountable to continuous learning and growth, and energy is renewed.

At our last debriefing session, the questions are still flowing. It's now 3:30 in the afternoon, and we have been debriefing since noon. The waiter looks anxious for us to leave, but nobody in the group seems ready to disband. We finally pay the bill, gather our things, and head toward the door. We're on our way.

Coaching Toward Implementation

Coach vt (1849) **1.** *to train intensively*
(as by instruction and demonstration).

—*Webster's Ninth New Collegiate Dictionary*

My fourth graders crowd onto the carpet in front of the rocking chair, and Marjory waits until they are settled. She holds a sack of markers, and by her side is a book bag full of her favorite titles. I sit nearby with a pen and notebook balanced on my lap. Today Marjory will teach a demonstration lesson, and together we will learn about reading comprehension strategies.

Marjory asks my fourth graders, "What do you think good readers do?"

Mayra raises her hand and responds with confidence, "They sound out the words."

Marjory nods her head. "Sure, decoding the words is an important part of reading, but I'm wondering what readers think about while reading."

This stumps them, but Marjory is ready. "I am going to read you one of my favorite stories by Sandra Cisneros. It's called 'Eleven' [1991]. What I want you to do is think about what pops into your head as you listen. Then, after I finish the story, we will make a list of everything we noticed ourselves thinking."

She begins reading, stopping every few minutes to think aloud. She models the questions and connections she has when reading "Eleven," such as memories of her own birthday. As I listen, I jot a few things down in my notebook. Then she finishes the story, looks up, and asks, "So, what did you notice?"

Anita answers, "I wondered why the story kept saying the same words."

Miguel adds, "I thought about what the girl's sweater looked like."

Mario says, "I remembered one time when a teacher embarrassed me in class."

"All good answers," Marjory responds. "You are starting to be 'metacognitive' while you read."

In my notebook I scribble, "What is metacognitive?"

She says, "Let's make a list of what we thought about as we read." On the chart paper behind her she jots down the following:

- we asked questions;
- we visualized; and
- we remembered something from our life that was similar to the story.

Then she says, "This year we are going to learn about what good readers think about, and we will probably add a lot more to this list. But for now I am going to ask Mrs. Sweeney if it is okay if we hang up this list so we can come back to it later."

I close my notebook as she finishes up the lesson. We sit down for our debriefing session while the students head to lunch.

"I hadn't really thought about all the things I think about as I read," I say. "It's incredible. I was impressed that the kids were able to come up with a few examples."

Marjory agrees: "It was a great start. Now I think we can really begin to focus on one of the strategies on their list."

"Aren't there seven comprehension strategies?" I ask. "What about the rest, and where do you think we should go from here?"

"You're right," Marjory says. "There are more strategies, but since this was the first time they were introduced, I thought we could begin with the ones they came up with. We'll get to the rest as we go. From here, I think we should focus on the strategy that Mario mentioned, which I call 'prior knowledge.'"

Marjory suggests a few things I could try until she returns to my classroom the following week. We decide that next time she will model how she explicitly teaches kids to use their prior knowledge when they read. I still have a lot of questions but feel confident they will get answered with time. The best part is knowing she will be back soon, and that I won't have to face implementation alone.

Marjory returns a few days later. Once again, she does the teaching while I observe. This time she reads *Smoky Night* by Eve Bunting (1994) and models her thinking. As she reads, she writes her thinking on sticky notes while we listen and watch. She shares thoughts such as, "My cat sometimes runs away, too," and "I remember hearing about the Los Angeles riots on television." Then she closes the book, looks up, and asks, "Do you think you might be able to read and jot down your thinking like I just did?" We nod our heads. "My challenge to you is to choose a book and try this out on your own. When I return, I can't wait to see what ideas you came up with."

As my instructional coach Marjory models the process of teaching reading comprehension and then offers me feedback when I try new things on my own. Without her, my implementation would most likely fail because I wouldn't have enough support to get there. Not only is she helping me become a better teacher, but she is building a shared understanding schoolwide because the lessons she teaches in my classroom are similar to those that she does for my colleagues. She is careful to use the same terminology with kids and teachers so our entire school community will develop a common language around the reading comprehension strategies. Kindergartners are learning to use the strategies just like my fourth graders, and the charts she creates hang in every classroom. With her help, we are finally able to create a consistent literacy curriculum.

Because the link is clear between teacher learning and student performance, instructional coaches are becoming more and more common in today's schools. Title I and special education programs now advocate supporting struggling students with coaching rather than the pull-out programs that existed in the past. With the elimination of pull-out programs, teachers are being supported in ways they never have been before.

Like most schools, Harrington originally offered a pull-out model. I kept a schedule pinned to my bulletin board that rivaled the complexity of a New York City bus schedule. In keeping with the pull-out model, many of my struggling students did a daily march down the hall to their Title I or special education classes. Martin left for Title I at 9:25 and returned at 10:15. Yadira headed to Title I at 11 and returned at 11:45. Manuel went to special education from 12:50 to 1:45. And just as he returned, Paula left.

I don't doubt that the special education and Title I teachers wanted the best for these students. The problem was one of accountability and raised the question, "Who really is responsible for these students' literacy instruction?" Is it the classroom teacher, even though the student is gone for half of the literacy block? Is it the Title I teacher who spends only forty minutes a day with the student? Or is it the special education teacher? Even worse, none of the concerned teachers regularly discussed the students or the curriculum. There was no rhyme or reason, and no common language or philosophy among the teachers. And as one might imagine, the students were not showing improvement.

In 1997, Harrington converted to schoolwide Title I. We knew we had to figure out a more supportive way to address the needs of our struggling students, so we began by eliminating three pull-out positions. This wasn't an easy sell. Although many of the teachers found the pull-out model limiting, others found it quite acceptable. These were hard kids to teach, kids who needed a lot of one-on-one support, and some teachers were relieved when they left the classroom for even a few minutes. We knew that we couldn't take away the support that pull-outs provided without replacing them with something better, and that is where instructional coaches came in. Whereas pull-out teachers mysteriously worked with our struggling students in closet-size classrooms down the hall, instructional coaches were in the classrooms with the teachers and their students. The teachers never knew what occurred during the pull-out instruction, and now they worked with their instructional coaches to better teach challenging students. Charmaine became a full-time math coach, I took the position as full-time literacy coach, and Marjory did both. Each of us targeted a different set of grade levels and began by working on a volunteer basis.

Discussion

One of the tasks for instructional coaches is leading teachers in discussion. Sally figured that if the teachers weren't trying new things in their classrooms, maybe they would learn from talking with people who were.

As you might imagine, finding the time to gather teachers to talk proved to be a challenge. Each grade level had a different lunch and planning period, and off-site classes and meetings were held after school. Before school, teachers were focused on getting ready for the day, and then there was playground duty. Both grade-level teams and the whole teaching staff needed time to talk, and we needed to think creatively about how to bring teachers together during the school day. Sally provided discussion through staff development meetings, grade-level planning sessions, teacher release for professional development, debriefing, and text-based discussion.

She began by changing the focus of faculty meetings from announcing school business to providing professional development. The staff development meetings rotated between math and literacy, and were facilitated by the instructional coaches. Charmaine brought problem-solving activities for the teachers to work on, shared new uses for math manipulatives, and helped everyone think about math in new ways. In the literacy meetings, we asked teachers to read and use the comprehension strategies, helped everyone continue to be better teachers of writing, and trained the teachers in literacy assessments. Most important, we used the time to talk about instruction.

In the past, each grade level had a different planning time, which made collaboration nearly impossible. We had fifty minutes of daily enrichment that included technology, integrated arts, library, and physical education, but with more than 500 students in grades K–5, rearranging the schedule seemed daunting. We began by rotating the teachers from a grade level through daily enrichment classes at the same time each day. Violà, we had grade-level planning time, but that wasn't enough. Even with the same planning time, some of the teachers continued to stay isolated, and it became evident that the culture hadn't changed as easily as the schedule had.

It wasn't until Sally decided to use the instructional coaches to facilitate the grade-level planning meetings that the meetings became productive. With the instructional coaches as facilitators, the meetings occurred weekly and were grounded in instructional strategies, assessments, and student work. Since the grade-level meetings were more intimate than the whole-staff meetings, they offered the opportunity for an in-depth sharing of ideas about day-to-day instruction as well as time for feedback, a key element of the guided practice phase on the gradual release continuum.

By the second year, grade-level meetings were an established part of the schedule. It took time to get teachers to see their value, with some still resenting the fact that they lost fifty minutes of planning time every week, but those who were most resistant ended up advocating planning together after they had experienced the benefits of the conversations.

In the effort to increase the time teachers spent collaborating, Sally also received grant funding for a program that brought certified art teachers into classrooms. While the art teachers rotated throughout the school, instructional coaches worked with vertical teams of teachers. It is all too easy for a first-grade teacher to say, "That kindergarten teacher didn't do her job," and it is important to avoid creating insular teams without a knowledge or understanding of the other grade levels. Vertical team discussion encouraged us to break down those grade-level barriers.

Think about a rushed visit at your doctor's office. There are always those questions you anticipate getting answers to, such as, "Why do I have a slight twinge in my knee?" or "Why have I been so tired lately?" Instead of taking the time to talk things over, he shoos you on your way, and you leave without the answers you hoped for. Neglecting a debriefing session leaves the teacher feeling like she has just walked out of a doctor's office. She might have a good idea for one fifty-minute lesson, but might not understand the lesson's purpose or where to go next. Instructional coaches provide opportunities for discussion after every demonstration lesson. Without an unhurried conversation afterward, both the teacher and instructional coach leave with unanswered questions, and the power of the lesson is greatly diminished.

With Marjory came the expectation that teachers read professional books and articles on a regular basis. Receiving articles from journals with "FYI, Marjory" scrawled in the corner became routine. Sometimes the articles were specific to whatever I was working on with my students, and sometimes an article was shared with the whole staff. She brought readings to our staff meetings, and we discussed them in small groups. She brought them to the classroom when she did a demonstration lesson, and she purchased books to be placed in a professional development library for teachers. To this day, I refer to the reading I did then, and now I share some of the same articles with other teachers.

Practical Steps

Instructional coaching supports teachers at any stage in their teaching career. It can include

1. *Observation with feedback.* Observation is a useful way to get to know the students as well as the teachers' style and interests, and even though feedback can be uncomfortable for both the observed and observer, it is the best way to determine the focus for future learning.

   As a staff developer, I always begin the coaching relationship with an observation. At the beginning, these observations don't usually carry a specific focus, but are more about developing a relationship with the teacher and students. As I observe the students and teacher, I take notes on a possible focus for professional development. During my debriefing session with the teacher, we talk about the positive things I saw in the classroom, and I always ask what areas he or she would like to focus on during our time together. By the end of the debriefing session, we know each other better and have defined where we want to go next. Even though the first observation can be unnerving for a teacher, it is a critical first step. Before we decide what new learning we want to engage in, I have to see where the teacher already is. I will no longer work with a teacher without an initial observation, because effective staff development is geared toward the individual needs of the teacher, and to know the teacher's needs you have to spend time in the classroom.

   Later on, the staff developer and teacher might decide together on a focus for the observation. Maybe the teacher wants feedback about whether he or she asks the students appropriate questions, or it could be that the teacher would like to have a lesson scripted to reflect on the language he or she uses. Observation is a powerful way to offer teachers feedback specific to their needs while creating a more effective relationship between the teacher and the instructional coach.

2. *Demonstration lessons.* One of the most effective tools for the modeling phase on the gradual release continuum, the demonstration lesson has three vital components: planning, the lesson itself, and the debriefing session.

Each component is vital to ensure that a demonstration lesson is productive.

When planning a demonstration lesson, the staff developer meets with the teacher beforehand to discuss what the teacher has tried, what challenges he or she has run up against, and what he or she wants to accomplish with the lesson.

Then, the demonstration lesson is just that: a lesson taught by the staff developer to demonstrate a curricular area and/or a teaching technique while the teacher observes. Even though the lesson is taught to the teacher's students, the main goal is for the teacher to learn. Sure, the students can't help but learn along the way, but the emphasis is on what new ideas the teacher walks away with.

During debriefing, the teacher has the opportunity to ask questions, share insights, and plan for next steps. Many times, debriefing focuses on the content of the lesson, what the students did, the resources that were used, and unanticipated successes or problems that occurred.

3. *Coteaching.* Once rapport and trust are established between the teacher and instructional coach, a natural next step is coteaching. Think of coteaching as the guided practice phase on the gradual release of responsibility continuum. After instruction is modeled, it is time for the teacher to try it in a supported environment. Just as with the demonstration lesson, there are three components to an effective coteaching experience: planning, the lesson itself, and debriefing. Planning the lesson is crucial. Without time to plan, coteaching fails to represent both the teacher and the instructional coach. Instead, the lesson begins with each person thinking differently about what will happen, and the experience no longer gives the teacher the opportunity to test his or her wings. Just like any professional development experience, debriefing is the last step so that the teachers have the opportunity to discuss how the lesson went and what their next steps might be.

Scheduling Using a Volunteer Approach

Just as with anything new, some teachers eagerly came on board while others waited in the wings, muttering, "This is like everything else. In a few years, we will be on to something different." Knowing this, the instructional coaches took a volunteer approach and began working with the teachers who expressed an interest, waiting to reach the teachers who were more reticent.

We resisted the temptation to assign teachers to work with an instructional coach. This might seem counterintuitive and too indirect, but put yourself in the place of the assigned teacher and think about how you would feel if an instructional coach showed up in your classroom because you had been deemed a below-par teacher. This not only puts the coach and teacher in an uncomfortable position but also detracts from building a community of learners where all parties can feel safe and supported. If the instructional coach is a valued commodity, then teachers will join in when they are ready. If some teachers never join in, I would question whether they want to be a part of the learning community in the first place.

Luckily, our volunteer approach was a hit, and most of the teachers were interested in working with us in their classrooms. But that meant we had to allocate our time across several teachers, which was close to impossible. Some asked to work with us every day, and others were more interested in time for collaborative planning. When allocating my time, I turned to the teachers with a survey (see Figure 4.1). It gave teachers a way to reflect upon and communicate their needs with me. Then I used their responses to create my schedule.

I created a new schedule four times each year. That way I could make myself available to those who had missed out previously. I was careful to work with teachers two to three times a week. Mondays were reserved for grade-level meetings, and we planned individually on Fridays. And even though the focus

Figure 4.1 Teacher Survey

Teacher name: _____

Block of time you need me: _____

Soon we will begin a new quarter, so it's time for me to check in to see how I can support your literacy instruction for the next ten weeks. Please check the area where you need the most help, and I will make every effort to get you on my schedule. Remember, I build my schedule as the surveys are turned in, so don't delay!
Thanks, Diane

I need help with

_____ teaching a single comprehension strategy (circle one: schema, asking questions, sensory images, determining importance, inferring, monitoring understanding, or synthesizing text);
_____ blending the comprehension strategies;
_____ teaching a particular genre (circle one: poetry, nonfiction, fiction, memoir, other _____);
_____ organizing reading instruction to include whole-group, small-group, and one-on-one instruction;
_____ assessing reading with reading inventories;
_____ organizing writing instruction;
_____ writing in a specific genre (circle one: poetry, nonfiction, fiction, memoir, other _____).
other:

Figure 4.2 My Schedule as an Instructional Coach

	Monday	Tuesday	Wednesday	Thursday	Friday
April–June 2000					
9:00–9:50	Susan Levy—working on comprehension	Lisi Quinby—working on fluency	Susan Levy—working on comprehension	Lisi Quinby—working on fluency	Susan Levy—working on comprehension
10:00–10:50	Sue Moening—working on comprehension	Lesley Bowman—working on organizing reading block	Sue Moening—working on comprehension	Lesley Bowman—working on organizing reading block	Irene Ribera—working on comprehension
10:50–11:30	3rd grade planning meeting	Christina Jensen—working on poetry	Christina Jensen—working on poetry	Christina Jensen—working on poetry	Plan with Alyssa
11:30–12:20	Lunch	Lunch	Lunch	Lunch	Lunch
12:20–1:10	One-on-One Planning	One-on-One Planning	One-on-One Planning	One-on-One Planning	One-on-One Planning
1:10–2:00	1st grade planning meeting	Alyssa Winnick—working on comprehension	Alyssa Winnick—working on comprehension	Alyssa Winnick—working on comprehension	Plan with Susan and Keith
2:00–2:50	2nd grade planning meeting	Plan with Rhonda	Kelli Woodrow—working on comprehension	Kelli Woodrow—working on comprehension	Plan with Lesley and Sue
3:00–3:30	My Planning	My Planning	My Planning	My Planning	My Planning

was specific to each teacher's needs, it always connected back to the schoolwide vision about literacy instruction (see Figure 4.2).

Tips for Instructional Coaches
- *Move forward only after establishing trust and rapport.* Most teachers are used to working behind closed doors, and working with an instructional coach can feel like a personal intrusion. As I mentioned earlier, teachers tend to be hard on themselves, and collaborating with a coach sometimes brings those insecurities to the surface. Coaches need to honor these fears. It is a matter of pushing a little, but not too hard. Listen to the teacher,

and don't try to fix everything at once. As a coach, choosing a focus for professional development can be overwhelming. Take your cues from the teacher, take your time, and take a deep breath.

- *Help teachers move through the gradual release continuum.* Sometimes teachers resist moving out of the modeling phase. The reason behind this is simple: the modeling phase involves less risk taking because most of the responsibility lies with the staff developer. In the guided-practice phase, more responsibility lies with the teacher, which can be scary because some teachers prefer for their practice to remain private, don't like to hear constructive criticism, and don't want anyone to see what they are doing until they are doing it perfectly. Moving into the guided-practice phase means the teacher has to take on new risks, an essential part of learning.

- *Work with a manageable number of teachers.* Many instructional coaches and/or principals think it isn't fair if they don't work with all the teachers, all the time. It takes a lot of drops to fill a bucket, and sometimes it can be more effective to work with fewer teachers, more days a week, and for fewer weeks, than to spread yourself across all teachers and grade levels. Dialogue with the whole staff can happen during grade-level planning or whole-staff meetings. Classroom coaching can be targeted to specific groups of teachers for several weeks at a time.

- *Meet with teachers frequently.* For instructional coaching to take hold, it should occur on a regular basis. Most teachers appreciate a consistent schedule, so arrange your schedule to include two or three days a week with each teacher. Popping into the classroom every once in awhile can be more frustrating than it is helpful.

- *Place value on planning and debriefing.* Plan and debrief with teachers on a regular basis. Avoid counting on time for this outside the school day, because competing with teachers' personal lives is yet another way to frustrate them. Some are willing to meet after school, but others have children to pick up, meetings to attend, or other obligations they shouldn't be asked to compromise. It is also important for coaches to set the example that this time together is important, and they should come prepared to make the time meaningful.

- *Make suggestions for improvement while still honoring the teacher.* Just like when we confer with students, find a positive for every negative and work with the teacher to decide upon one area at a time to focus on. Learning takes time, and we have to remember that this is true for adults as well as children. It is easy for teachers to feel overwhelmed, so it is the job of the instructional coach to keep the teacher's comfort level in mind while helping him or her move forward.

- *Encourage and model note taking.* Sometimes it is helpful to give teachers a place to take notes. Give teachers professional development notebooks, a place to jot down their thoughts and ideas during planning, during the lessons they observe, and during the debriefing sessions. The coach can model note taking by being an active note-taker herself or by modeling a structure that will help teachers keep their notes organized and focused. (See Figure 4.3 for an example of a note-taking form.)

- *Use an open-ended approach when debriefing.* To hear from the teachers, get them talking. Allow for wait time, because some of us need more time to process our thoughts. If the teacher seems stymied, it may help to take a few minutes to write personal reflections. With time, the relationship will develop, and the conversation will flow more smoothly. (For some examples of conversational starters, see Figure 4.4.)

- *Allay teachers' fears about student behavior.* The first reaction of many teachers when working with an instructional coach is to worry about student behavior. Talk about this with the teacher before beginning work in the classroom. If a teacher is overly concerned with behavior, she will

Figure 4.3 Note-Taking Form

Date:
Lesson Focus:

Big question that was generated in the planning session:

Resources for the lesson such as book titles and other materials:

What you observed during the lesson:

What questions you still have after the lesson:

What you plan to do next:

Figure 4.4 Conversational Starters

What did you think . . .
Tell me more about . . .
How does this meet your needs?
What are you wondering about?
What have you noticed about your students?
What's on your mind?

What progress are you seeing?
What have you tried on your own?
What continues to challenge you?
What successes have you had?
Where do you want to go next?
What can I do for you?
What do you need next?

---

likely miss the instruction that is being modeled. Most coaches are experienced teachers who can easily handle whatever behavior problems come up, so encourage the teacher to focus on the lesson and remember that this time is for the teacher, not the students.

- *Be clear about the purpose of the lesson before the lesson begins.* If the teacher and coach plan together, the purpose of the lesson will be clear from the beginning. If the purpose isn't clear, then question whether the lesson is well timed.

- *Combine debriefing and planning sessions as long as enough meeting time has been allocated.* A combined debriefing/planning session typically lasts thirty to forty-five minutes. The first phase is discussing the lesson that was just taught. Questions such as, "What did you think?" and "What questions do you have?" are good starters for this part of the conversation. Then it is time to discuss next steps. A guiding question might be, "Where do you want to go from here?" After next steps have been talked over, it is time to plan the next lesson. By this time, you will have a large list of potential next steps, so this part of the planning phase is settling on one. A question for this part of the conversation might be, "Since I am going to be back in your classroom on Wednesday, which one of these ideas would you like me to focus on in my demonstration lesson?" To wrap up, you will have various details to talk over: which resources you will use, when the lesson will take place, and what the focus will be.

- *Be metacognitive during demonstration lessons.* Don't get so involved in the demonstration lesson that you forget to stop and clarify your thinking with the classroom teacher. Share your thinking about why you chose the book you are using, what you think the students will be able to produce when they begin working independently, why you are charting particular ideas, and anything else that comes to mind. Teachers learn more quickly when they understand why you are doing what you are doing.

A Final Thought

Ligia, a friend and teacher at Harrington, once compared the instructional coach to a bumblebee flitting around a school and cross-pollinating ideas from teacher to teacher. I had never thought of it that way but it's true: instructional coaches customize professional development to match each teacher's needs and interests while they help a school establish a common understanding across all teachers. Bees have a distinct and well-understood set of goals, and with the help of instructional coaches, teachers can, too.

Part

Guided Practice

After exemplary instruction has been modeled, teachers need support in adapting what they observed to their own classrooms. No two classrooms or teachers are alike, so implementing what has been observed is a highly individualistic endeavor. In the guided-practice phase, staff developers work alongside teachers to offer the feedback that is essential to teacher learning. In this section, Chapter 5 examines the different ways adults process new information, and Chapter 6 suggests examining student work as a means of determining next steps in instruction.

Chapter 5

Processing New Information to Make It Your Own

Information's pretty thin stuff unless mixed with experience.

—Clarence Day

Keith leads his tiny children up the stairs on this fall morning. Like the Pied Piper, he stands in front while his children diligently follow. As they enter the classroom, Keith quietly reminds them to put their backpacks away before joining him on the carpet. The desks are at shin level and the chairs are too small to hold most adults. Bright sunlight streams into the classroom through the west-facing windows, and the students wear tank tops and shorts because of the unusually warm weather. Around the classroom are plastic bins filled with books for emergent readers. A large calendar hangs in the corner and in front sits a rocking chair. Without saying a word, Keith settles into the rocking chair while his students begin gathering at his feet.

As an instructional coach, I have spent a lot of time in classrooms and a question I commonly ask myself is, "Would I want to be a student here?" When it comes to Keith's classroom, the answer is a resounding yes. It's 1999, and Keith is new to the school but not new to teaching. He transferred to Harrington from another school in the district, and everyone feels lucky.

When you consider the range of teacher expertise at a typical school, you'll find teachers who have been there for years, teachers fresh out of a teacher preparation program, teachers like Keith who have experience in other places, and everything in between. Along with all of these differences, teacher learners move through the same gradual release continuum in their own way and accord-

53

ing to their own time line. If professional development is matched to individual learning styles, then the optimal learning conditions exist and learning will be accomplished—yet another reason for a professional development model that meets the varying needs of teachers.

Even though Keith is an experienced teacher, he still needs staff development so he can be integrated into Harrington's school culture and philosophy. Every Friday afternoon, Keith and I spend forty-five minutes planning for the following week. We share what the students are working on, where they have struggled, and where to go next. Keith's teammate and sidekick, Susan, is a part of our planning meetings. She is in her first year teaching and is already riding high on her successes. By chance, Keith and Susan ended up on the same team, and just a few weeks into the year, they are already fast friends.

The glazed-over look of exhaustion, typical of first-grade teachers on Friday afternoons, has set in. The three of us sit around a table in Susan's classroom. Everyone is tired, but we realize we'd better plan now.

Susan says, "You know, my kids are really catching on to the strategy of self-questioning; the only thing is, their questions are on the surface, and I think we need to work with them on how to ask better ones."

Keith nods and adds, "It took a long time to get my students to even ask questions, and I want to be careful not to discourage them."

"When I was working on my master's degree," Susan says, "we did some work with dramatic improvisation, and I think that might come in handy here. We could have the students do dramatic improvisation while the others ask them questions, sort of like peer conferences." Then she throws in, "But do you think we could pull off tying self-questioning into dramatic improvisation, and do you think it would benefit their reading?"

Keith's wheels are spinning, and he says, "I have always wanted to teach my kids to have more productive peer conferences. When they read each other's stories, all they know how to say is, 'I liked it.' Maybe this way we could work with them to ask questions that move the writer's, or actor's, thinking."

We spend the next thirty minutes brainstorming and decide to start with dramatizing poetry. I ask how I can help them get it rolling and Susan suggests I come into her classroom to coteach a lesson about asking deeper questions. Keith feels confident about trying what we have discussed on his own, knowing that we will come together exhausted and ready to plan in a week's time.

Though they work well as a team, are good friends, and teach in a similar style, Susan and Keith process information differently. During our planning sessions, Susan has a lot to say. She thinks aloud and fires off questions. Keith sits quietly and lets her take center stage. He rarely asks questions, but when he does, they are thoughtful and demonstrate that he is thinking deeply and making connections to his practice. Susan processes verbally and through discussion, whereas Keith processes by putting what we talked about into action. Whereas Susan does her best learning in the planning session itself, Keith learns through implementation.

Most professional development offers little opportunity for information processing. When teachers sit through an entire inservice that consists of a person talking in the front of the room, they are on their own to process the information. Too often the planners assume that the teachers will be able to return to their classrooms and directly apply what they heard. These learners are few and far between, making most of the information inaccessible to the majority of teachers in attendance.

Learning is an individual pursuit, and a one-size-fits-all approach can't work. This chapter will look closely at how adult learners process information to successfully move through the gradual release continuum. You will have the opportunity to consider the kind of learner you are by using a variety of surveys and tools, and I will share how Harrington's professional development model meets the needs of all learners.

Dunn and Dunn on Processing Styles

Kenneth and Rita Dunn (1999) have given much thought to processing styles. Their work is based on feedback from thousands of teachers and students and is broken down into two main categories: *global* and *analytic processors.*

According to Dunn and Dunn, global processors tend to be more random. They function better when goals are general and include multiple approaches and options. They work best in environments that offer background noise, music, and conversation, and prefer an informal agenda with opportunities for short breaks. Global processors also work best when tackling simultaneous projects. When putting together a piece of furniture a global processor might say, "I never read the directions because it takes too much time."

Analytic processors prefer working toward a clear set of objectives and are interested in reaching specific conclusions or outcomes. They appreciate a quiet environment and a formal agenda. Analytics tend to persist with few breaks and feel more comfortable tackling a single project at a time. An analytic might say, "I can't get anything done until I get organized."

Global and analytic processors approach all of life's tasks differently and need learning that adapts to their distinct needs. When it comes to professional development global processors aren't happy when faced with successive teaching, a rigid and inflexible schedule, minimal peer activity, or listening for a long time. Analytics, on the other hand, become frustrated with humor and stories without objectives, too much noise or distraction, being forced into groups when they would rather work alone, disorganized and unclear directions, or being left on their own without handouts.

When considering the differences between global and analytic processors, we are once again reminded of the challenge of putting together professional development that meets every teacher's needs.

A short while into a math inservice, Keith passes a note to Susan: "What is she talking about?"

The presenter doesn't notice and jabbers on, "I'm from Minnesota, and you probably know our governor is Jessie Ventura. Well, I brought my Jessie Ventura doll to show you." She holds up a doll dressed in combat fatigues that resembles ex-wrestler Jessie "The Body" Ventura. Susan writes back, "I can't believe she is showing us dolls. What does this have to do with math?" The note passing and unrelated stories continue for the rest of the morning, and as the hours tick by, Keith and Susan become more and more frustrated. They are being held captive in what Dunn and Dunn call the circle of unhappiness. Some people in the room are happy to hear the storytelling, and a few even join in, but the analytics are fed up.

Other Processing Styles

Beyond Dunn and Dunn's globals and analytics, I have observed some other styles of information processing. Though most learners lean toward a single style, some are *integrated* and can operate in a wide variety of processing modes. I use the terms *verbal processors, writers, adapter/appliers,* and *visualizers.*

Verbal processors prefer open agendas and extended periods of time to meet and talk through ideas. They construct new understanding as they go and value input from others. At Harrington, verbal processors have ample time to work through their latest dilemma or challenge in grade-level meetings, planning sessions, book clubs, and study groups.

Writers process more effectively through written reflections. They are less comfortable throwing ideas out to a group before they have had time to think them over privately. At Harrington, writing is a part of observations and debriefing sessions. At these times, teachers are encouraged to record their observations, reflections, and questions. When time is included for written reflection, the writers in the group appreciate the gift of a few quiet moments to think and reflect.

Adapter/appliers process by recreating new information to meet their needs. At Harrington, adapter/appliers have many opportunities to individualize new learning because there are no formulas or demands for exact replication. Instead they take what they are given, change it for their own particular use, and share their new ideas with their peers.

Visualizers are challenged when they are expected to absorb new information without a visual picture. They process through visualizing and become frustrated when new ideas are shared in a lecture format. These are the learners who benefit least from the inservice approach. Instead, they depend on in-classroom demonstrations, videos, and other visual pictures to make their learning real. The modeling phase of the gradual release of responsibility model is key for these learners.

The early morning quiet gives way to the noise of bells and children. The daily ritual is the mad rush to the rest room one last time before we start our morning lessons. I run in, dump my armful of books, and am relieved to see that there is an empty stall. Then I hear Susan's voice from the other side of the barrier. "Diane, is that you? I wanted to talk to you about what poem you think I should use today for our improvisation lesson. I was thinking we did Shel Silverstein the last few times, and the kids loved it. But I am wondering if we shouldn't do a more serious poem. I would hate to give them the impression that all poems are silly. What do you think?"

We talk over options, from stall to stall. Flush. I laugh while pointing out, "You know, Susan, that is my first planning session in a bathroom."

Susan is a verbal processor. She feels compelled to talk over her lesson ideas and the work her students are producing, or just to think aloud about her teaching decisions. She needs a lot of one-on-one attention, and as her instructional coach, I have to be careful to schedule my time with her accordingly. After all, we can't survive on bathroom meetings alone. When I create my schedule, I schedule time with Susan at least four days a week. Much of our time together is during her literacy block, and the rest is our weekly planning sessions. Keith, on the other hand, doesn't need nearly as much time and attention. We meet weekly, and I spend time in his classroom whenever he expresses a need. At first I worried that I was selling him short, but as I got to know him as a learner, I realized that this is the way he operates best.

Giving Learners Time to Process

To move through each phase on the gradual release continuum, learners need time. The complexity of the task itself affects processing time and there are unlimited examples of complex tasks for teaching. Consider building a literate classroom environment or organizing small reading groups; both are examples of complex tasks that teachers can't be expected to learn overnight. No matter what the learners' processing style, they need time to see the process modeled, to practice with feedback, and to maintain independence.

Another factor may be the match between learner style and the delivery of professional development. The task will be accomplished more quickly if there is a match. For example, if a visualizer participates in professional development such as observing in a lab classroom, learning will occur readily. If, however, the visualizer does not have opportunities to observe, learning may take longer.

Learning is also affected by the amount and quality of support offered throughout the gradual release continuum. Support may come in the form of coaching, team meetings, follow-up sessions, or reading and discussing professional books or articles. After the information has been shared, time is set aside to refine and support teachers' efforts in applying what has been discussed, an essential part of the gradual release continuum.

Every type of learner needs time to process new information. Verbal processors need time to talk over ideas, preferably in small groups; writers need time alone to reflect; and adapter/appliers need to tinker before starting implementation. The common thread is time.

Keith explains how it feels to be forced to process too quickly. "I get frustrated when I am at a meeting and they give us paper after paper after paper to read, read, read, read, read. We never have time to discuss it, go try it, or come back to talk about it. It's like it's just a way to say, 'We dealt with this—check it off the list and move on to the next thing.' I think this works for a certain type of learner, but for me, it doesn't. It's overwhelming."

Every learner, whether big or small, needs processing time. If true learning is the goal, you can't rush it. Consider what the anticipated outcome is, and remember that for some people, the learning may be brand new. In that case the expert needs to step back and consider the learners who have never heard this before. The key is figuring out a way for all learners to access the information, and that usually means modeling, guided practice, and time for processing.

Practical Steps

Encourage teachers to self-assess to define their best learning style, using Dunn and Dunn's categories of globals and analyzers, my verbal processors, writers, adapters/appliers, and visualizers, or the categories by Honey and Mumford (1982) in Figure 5.1. Then, work together to design professional development that meets every teacher's needs.

Figure 5.1 Individual Learning Styles

If your preference is for the following style . . .	You will learn best from activities in which . . .	You will learn least from activities in which . . .
Activist	—there are new experiences/problems/opportunities from which to learn —there is excitement/drama/crisis and things change with a range of diverse activities to tackle —you are involved with other people, i.e., bouncing ideas off them, solving problems as part of a team	—learning involves a passive role, i.e., listening to lectures, monologues, explanations, statements of how things should be done, reading, or watching —you are required to assimilate, analyze, and interpret lots of (messy) data —you have precise instructions to follow with little room to maneuver
Reflector	—you are able to stand back from events and listen/observe, i.e., observing a group at work, taking a backseat at a meeting, or watching a video —you are asked to produce carefully considered analyses or reports —you can reach a decision in your own time without pressure and tight deadlines	—you are forced into the limelight, i.e., to act as a leader/chairman, to role play in front of onlookers —you are given cut-and-dried instructions on how things should be done —you are involved in situations that require action without planning
Theorist	—what is being offered is part of a system, model, concept, or theory —you are intellectually challenged with analyzing a complex situation —you are teaching high-caliber people who ask searching questions —you can analyze and then generalize reasons for success and failure	—you are pitched into using or doing something without a context or apparent purpose —you find the subject matter shallow or gimmicky
Pragmatist	—there is an obvious link between the subject matter and a problem or opportunity —you have the opportunity to try out and practice techniques with coaching/feedback from a credible source —you are given immediate opportunities to implement what you have learned	—organizers of the learning seem distant from reality, i.e., "ivory towered," all theory and general principles, or all "chalk and talk" —there is no practice and there are no clear guidelines on how to do it —there are political, managerial, or personal obstacles to implementation

Adapted from Honey and Mumford 1982

A Final Thought

My husband recently came home from a computer class, and headed right to his study. I peeked in the door to ask how the class went, and found him busily creating his first Web page. A few weeks later he was set to attend his second class, this time with the goal of mastering Excel software. When he came home, I asked, "So how was it?"

He groaned, "It was a four-hour class and I never even touched a keyboard! It felt like a waste of time." His first instructor taught him through application. The class was held in a room filled with computers, and the students worked through Web site development with the instructor's help. The second instructor lectured with a PowerPoint projector. Although each student sat at a computer, the instructor controlled the screens and never allowed the students a chance to apply what they were learning. Anyone who has used a computer knows that you don't learn by watching someone else do it. You learn by doing. The stark difference between my husband's computer classes brings home the importance of all that you read about in this chapter: remember the learner.

Chapter 6

Staying Grounded in Student Work

It's what we think we already know that
often prevents us from learning.

—Claude Bernard

Late in the spring I run into Jamie, a student from Cindy's classroom. Her smile stretches from ear to ear, and a ribbon of paper trails behind her. She has taped together the pages of her latest story, and she carries them high over her head, careful not to let her words touch the ground. Jamie isn't a typical ten-year-old. Her mother is in and out of jail, and she is in the care of a teenage sister. Jamie's hair is tightly braided into cornrows. A scowl is her typical expression and "Just try to make me do it" is her mantra. Even as a fourth grader, she intimidates most adults. Yet her proud strut down the school hallway, with her writing in hand, reveals another side of Jamie. Thanks to Cindy and writer's workshop, Jamie is willing to write because for the first time, Jamie chooses what she writes. For the first time, she makes the rules.

As happy as I am to see this transformation in Jamie, I wonder if we might have settled too quickly for such personal successes. We had spent a lot of time discussing our writing instruction, but we hadn't taken a close look at the work our students were producing as a whole. We celebrated the successes of individual students but failed to analyze the trends across students and grade levels. Our professional development is supportive and comfortable, but I realize our learning has stalled out. We need to come together to take a much closer look at our students' writing even though deep down we know we may not like what we see. Without knowing it, we haven't been engaging in the feedback that is essential to the guided-practice phase of professional development.

Grounding Professional Development in Student Work

Right around this time, Jamie and the rest of the fourth graders are about to struggle through the state-required writing assessment. Cindy passes out the test and her students begin writing. The test prompt reads, "Describe a typical day in your school cafeteria." Gerardo writes, "I hate the cafeteria because it's noisy." Amanda says, "My favorite is chocolate milk." Jamie scrawls, "I eat fast so I can go outside." Practically every fourth grader in the school responds to the prompt with an opinion, even though the correct response is to describe how the cafeteria functions. Those scoring the assessment are looking for something like, "The first thing I do is pick up my tray. Then I go through the line and choose my lunch." We soon realize our students only seem to know how to write their opinions.

This experience arouses our interest in figuring out ways to improve our students' writing, so the instructional coaches decide it is time to suggest that the grade-level teams spend some time analyzing student work. In our weekly staff development meeting Marjory explains, "We are going to compare our student writing to benchmark papers I have collected from schools that are scoring well on the state assessment. That way we will see where our students are not doing well. Everyone will write to the same prompt so we have something that is comparable—in other words, something that is written in the same genre and text structure. I suggest we begin with a prompt that is sequenced. We'll give the students a few weeks to write to the prompt and then come together in grade-level teams to see how they did."

"Writing to a prompt goes against everything I believe," Cindy protests. "I think my students should be able to choose what they write."

I help Marjory out by saying, "The prompts will be only one small part of our writing instruction. I agree that students should choose their own topics, but now that these writing assessments are a reality, we are trying to figure out where to go next with our learning so we can help our students with their learning."

More than anything the teachers are nervous. The benchmark papers Marjory collected are from schools in the suburbs. Schools where students are read to every night and never faced learning English as a second language. Schools where we assume teaching seems a whole lot easier. Even so, everyone agrees and we decide on our first prompt.

The prompt we select is "Describe your morning routine." Kindergartners draw and label their pictures with a few words. The fifth graders write in a paragraph format. A few teachers mention that they dread the day they will have to share their student work with the rest of their grade-level team. Will their peers pass judgment on their teaching ability when they share their students' work?

Will the teacher have the opportunity to explain how far some students have come, even though they have far to go? How much of a match will there be? Will the students' work be deemed proficient when measured against the benchmark? We will soon find out.

Grounding Professional Development in Student Work: A Risky Business

Two weeks have passed since we began working with the prompt, and it is time to analyze our first sample. Throughout the day, every grade-level team will meet with their instructional coach to analyze the pieces. Each team will have fifty minutes together, and we hope our students aren't too far off.

Since I provide instructional coaching for the first-grade team, I will help facilitate their conversation. Lisi, Christina, Keith, and Susan make their way into my office, and right away it is clear that they are worried about their students' performance with the prompt. "I hope I did this right," Christina admits. "I wasn't exactly sure how much help to give them."

I try to console her. "There isn't really a right or wrong way to do this. We are just here to look at the work and see what we find."

I ask the group who would like to share today, and Lisi volunteers to go first. She passes around copies of a piece by Javier, one of her emergent English speakers. Beforehand, the first-grade team had decided to help their students sequence the piece by folding the paper into six sections. That way, they thought, the task would be more concrete for the young writers.

In each section of his paper, Javier had written a sentence describing what he did in the morning. "I bruch teeth" was in the first box. Then, "I wach TV" in the second. He continued with an idea in each box and then finished with, "I go to scool."

We take a few moments to read over Javier's writing and Susan already has a question for Lisi. "How did you get him to write a different idea in each box? My students didn't seem to understand how to do that."

"Just like anything: I started by modeling the task," Lisi answers. "I wrote my own while they observed. Then we did a few together during shared writing. And finally, after these examples, they tried it on their own."

Susan says, "Of course. I should have known they needed to see it modeled so many times. I think I asked them to write too quickly."

Next we talk about how Javier jumped right into his piece without an introduction. We agree that this was confusing to the reader and decide to teach our students how to write an introduction. On the other hand, Javier ended the piece with a simple conclusion, and the rest of the first-grade teachers volunteer that most of their students hadn't done that. We all have the same opinion that Javier could use a few transition words to guide the reader through his sequence.

By the end of our meeting, we have a long list of next steps for our instruction. We decide to keep working on this one for another week, so the students can have help making their pieces better. Next week, we'll compare our students' pieces with the benchmark papers.

Until now teaching had been a private act and no one really knew how each others' students were doing, so it wasn't surprising that not every teacher bravely volunteered to share a student work sample. A few even openly complained that the meetings were a waste of time. I acknowledged that I was sorry they felt that way and reminded them that they didn't have to bring student work until they felt ready. As the first volunteers went through the process, a sense of trust was gradually established. Our conversations remained focused on what the student work was teaching us, and we were careful to honor the students, remembering that our goal was to improve our instruction. It didn't take long for the most reserved teachers to see the benefits of the conversations. After sitting through a few sessions and seeing the presenting teachers walk away with so many ideas, they decided they wanted the same support and volunteered to go next.

Looking together at student work fits into the guided-practice phase of the gradual release continuum. In many schools, this is brand new territory, because most teachers rarely expose their students' performance to colleagues. It's the masterpieces that get passed around; rarely does anything short of perfection hang on the bulletin board outside the classroom door, and planning with colleagues is more focused on next steps than on what the students are already doing.

Examining student work fits into all phases on the gradual release continuum. Modeling comes in the form of defining a standard for student writing. Just as observing good instruction helps teachers determine a set of goals for their instruction, looking at benchmark papers helps them determine a set of goals for student writing.

Conferring with students is the cornerstone for the guided-practice phase, because it gives teachers the opportunity to figure out next steps based on the students' needs. Similarly, grade-level meetings give me the opportunity to confer with the teachers I coach because discussing student work helps me see what they are doing well and where to go next.

Guided practice is also provided through my work in the teachers' classrooms. For example, when the teachers realized their first graders weren't writing introductions, I modeled that during the time I spent in their classrooms. When they wanted to model sequenced text, I helped them find books and other resources.

Support is also offered during professional development meetings. Together, the whole faculty discussed sequencing in different genres: "how to's" such as recipes, chronological sequencing in biographies and historical fiction, the way a letter is sequenced, and the types of transition words a writer uses to sequence a piece of writing. A conversation about sequencing began to permeate the school, and as teachers reached independence on the gradual release continuum, they had many opportunities to share. We were grounding professional development in the actual work our students produced instead of on instinct or philosophy.

In its early stages the process isn't easy, and it isn't long before we realize that our students aren't even close to the standards against which they are being measured. The benchmark papers from other schools reveal that a piece by a Harrington fourth grader roughly compares to the proficiency level of a second grader. After spending so much time with our own students we have no perspective on what even constitutes proficient writing. Reality is staring us in the face and we are overwhelmed. "How will we ever get them there?" "There's no way," and "That's a first grader's writing?" are the comments that fly around the room.

Comparing our students' writing with the benchmarks gives us the ambition to keep working on sequencing for a few more months. We use children's literature as well as nonfiction to model how other writers sequence text. Teachers write their own pieces to share with students, and students share their writing on a regular basis. By the second month, we begin to notice that our students are writing well-sequenced pieces, and that's when our focus changes.

"My kids can write sequenced pieces in their sleep, but they're boring. I think we need to help them write more descriptively," Paul complains to the other fourth-grade teachers at the grade-level meeting. "Does anyone else feel that way?" The other teachers agree, and we realize that having accomplished our first goal, it is time to help our students breathe more life into their writing. Descriptive writing becomes our focus. We find benchmark papers that are written descriptively, create prompts for the students to practice writing descriptive pieces, and continue to come together with our student work. This time around we are more comfortable, and everybody is willing to share his or her students' work. The fifty minutes always pass too quickly.

Practical Steps

When Harrington began looking at student work, we were casual in our approach. Since then, I have learned that a number of protocols are available to help formalize the process. In their bulletin, Phi Delta Kappan speaks to the genesis of looking at student work and Critical Friends Groups:

> The professional development unit of the Annenberg Institute for School Reform, the National School Reform Faculty (NSRF), took on the task of designing a program to train coaches who would help groups of practitioners, or Critical Friends Groups (CFG's), identify student learning goals that make sense in their schools, look reflectively at practices intended to achieve those goals, and collaboratively examine teacher and student work in order to meet their objectives. (*Phi Delta Kappan Research Bulletin*, December 2000, No. 28)

Here we were looking at student work while there were protocols designed to make the task easier and more effective.

In our experience, it was important to maintain a single focus during a Critical Friends Group. At Harrington, our focus was on teaching writing. With a single focus, the teachers knew what type of student work they would be examining. More important, the instructional coaches found it easier to provide support in the classrooms to follow up on the group's discoveries.

We also learned to ease into the process gradually. Looking at student work is intimidating for many teachers, so give teachers time to adjust to this new way of working together. Let the process evolve at its own rate. Give the group time to linger, and don't rush an outcome.

It is important to avoid letting too much time pass between sessions. We met every other week in grade-level teams, giving us enough time to do the work between sessions while still keeping the momentum going. The process takes time, so determine a regular schedule for meeting. If the meetings are anticipated, the teachers will have time to collect the student work they plan to present.

To create a shared experience we rotated presenters. Anyone who has had the chance to present a piece of student work in a Critical Friends Group knows what a powerful experience it can be. Make sure that everyone has the opportunity to present, but don't force those who might not be ready.

We also asked the presenting teacher to bring a copy of the student work for everyone in the group. The group will need time to carefully analyze the student piece before launching into a discussion, and the pieces can be archived in case the group wants to reexamine them at a later date.

Finally, we learned how important it is to come to the meetings with a nonjudgmental attitude. Questions are a critical part of these discussions, but a Critical Friends Group isn't the time to challenge or instruct the other teachers in the group. Maintain a spirit of neutral inquiry.

Establishing a Safe Community for Critical Friends Groups

Because a Critical Friends Group may be the first time a group of teachers comes together in this manner, it is a good idea to begin by defining how the group chooses to function as a learning community. Together group members brainstorm what they believe is important for their learning community. For example, our learning community will

- be safe;
- address the self-interests of group members;
- have a clear set of norms;
- have shared leadership;
- encourage mutual respect;
- provide time together, both productive and fun;
- have a shared vision that may need to be flexible;
- offer members the opportunity to really know each other;
- include rituals and celebrations; and
- respect differences and opinions of all group members.

It is also important to set group norms early on, because it is more awkward to deal with problems after they have occurred than to deal with them in advance through a norm-setting process. We set the following norms at the beginning:

- listen to each other;
- come with a nonjudgmental attitude;
- take charge of your own learning, and at the same time, honor the other learners in the group;
- consider all questions to be safe questions;
- avoid interrupting others;
- come ready to participate;
- do your homework.

Roles for Protocols

Each participant has a specific role in a Critical Friends Group. A single group member acts as facilitator to keep the discussion focused. The presenter(s) are responsible for bringing student work samples, or in some cases instructional dilemmas or teacher assignments. A process observer listens to the discussion and takes notes about how the group functioned. Responders offer feedback to

Figure 6.1 The Roles for Protocols

Roles	Tasks	Tips
Facilitator	—Guides the discussion —Ensures that the protocol is followed —Keeps track of time —Redirects conversation that gets off track —Attends to the focus question posed by the presenter	—Be assertive about the time. —Be sure no one monopolizes. —Invite quiet participants to join the conversation, but don't force comments. —Be protective of the presenter. Remember that when teachers make their work public, they are highly vulnerable. —Encourage provocative comments. Everyone should leave the conversation with a new or altered insight. —Encourage warm comments, but don't let all the comments stay on the warm side. —Seek divergent points of view. Ask if anyone sees the situation another way.
Presenter(s)	—Presents student work —Decides on the appropriate protocol —Frames a question —Listens and takes notes of comments —At the appropriate time, responds to the comments	—Select work that raises a question for you. —Take a risk; avoid "masterpieces." —Meet with the facilitator beforehand to frame your question. —Even when the group is on the wrong track when discussing your work, listen for new insights or for the reasons for misunderstanding. Sometimes what sends the group in a wrong direction is what also misdirects students.
Process Observer	—Notes the dynamics of the group —Provides a picture of how the group works together	—Watch who has the floor space and who doesn't. —Note who emerges as the leader. —Record the kind of comments made. —Attend to what can be observed rather than what can be inferred.
Responders	—Discuss the work —Provide feedback —Follow the protocol	—Be respectful of the presenter(s). Remember how vulnerable they are when they make their work public. —Contribute to substantive conversation. Keep in mind that we grow from understanding our strengths and from having a new understanding provoked. —Respect the time. —Invite quiet participants to join the conversation. —Encourage divergent points of view.

Adapted from Benson 2000

the presenting teacher(s). Literacy consultant Laura Benson created a list of roles, tasks, and tips that are helpful for clarifying the roles of participants (see Figure 6.1).

Probing Questions

Questioning techniques are important to consider when using protocols. In the following examples, questions are distinguished as *clarifying questions* and *probing questions*. Clarifying questions are factual and designed to help responders get a complete picture of the question, dilemma, or work sample that is being presented. Clarifying questions might be like these: What did you do before this particular lesson? What was your goal for the lesson? How many students do you have? What is the students' educational background? If the presenter has to think before answering, it is most likely a probing question rather than a question intended to clarify. Most protocols allow time for clarifying questions because getting enough background comes before the group brainstorms a solution.

Probing questions are more substantive and therefore are intended to help the group think more deeply about the dilemma. Learning to ask probing questions takes practice, and the National School Reform Faculty (NSRF) put *suggestions* and *probing questions* at either end of their questioning spectrum (see Figure 6.2).

According to the NSRF, the purpose for probing questions is to

- help uncover a belief rather than a solution;
- create depth in conversation;
- reinforce that we are creating a culture in which we can learn together;
- move the presenter into new territory;
- help move beyond the original perspective or insight; and
- lead to an "aha."

They also suggest that when constructing probing questions,

Figure 6.2 A Continuum of Questions

A Continuum of Questions		
Suggestions	Suggestions disguised	Probing
	as probing questions	questions

Adapted from the National School Reform Faculty

- prepare questions carefully before asking them;
- check to see if you have a "right" answer in mind. If so, delete judgment from the question or don't ask it;
- refer to the presenter's original question; and
- check to see if you are asserting your own agenda. If so, return to the presenter's agenda.

Examples of Protocols for Engaging in Discussion

When we began looking at student work at Harrington, we took an informal approach and didn't know there were research organizations, such as the National School Reform Faculty, the Annenberg Institute, and the Coalition of Essential Schools, that were developing protocols right under our noses. Now we know that these protocols would have made looking at student work both more comfortable and more focused.

Here are a few protocols that I have found to be particularly useful when working with teachers. They range in purpose from assessing student work against the standards to analyzing an open-ended dilemma. Though I am sharing only a few examples, others are available through the previously mentioned school reform organizations.

Connections Protocol

(taken from the Quaker tradition)
Purpose: This protocol is designed to encourage a safe community of learners by allowing group members to become more familiar with each other.
Time: approximately 10–15 minutes.

1. Facilitator introduces the protocol and reminds group members of the following expectations:
   - speak if you want to;
   - don't speak if you don't want to;
   - speak only once until everyone has had a chance to speak; and
   - listen and note what people say, but do not respond.
2. Facilitator opens Connections Protocol.
3. Responders say what is on their mind either personally or professionally.
4. When comments begin to subside, the facilitator warns that Connections Protocol will be closing soon.
5. After a few minutes the facilitator closes Connections Protocol.

Tuning Protocol

(adapted from MacDonald 1996)

Purpose: This protocol is designed to provide feedback on either a teacher's assignment or on student work.

Time: approximately 60 minutes.

1. Introduction (up to 3 minutes)
   - The facilitator introduces the protocol, time frame, and norms.
2. Presentation (7 minutes)
   - The presenting teacher explains a context and background for the work.
   - The presenting teacher shares what he would like addressed by asking the group a focus question.
   - Responders listen and take notes.
3. Clarifying questions (7 minutes)
   - Responders ask questions to clarify their understanding.
   - Clarifying questions are factual, straightforward, and nonjudgmental.
   - The presenting teacher answers clarifying questions without going into great detail.
   - Responders take notes.
4. Examination of student work samples (5 minutes)
   - The presenting teacher brings a copy of the student sample for every group member.
   - Responders silently read the work while keeping in mind the presenting teacher's earlier question.
5. Feedback (18–20 minutes)
   - The presenting teacher remains silent while the responders generate comments. They address issues such as the strengths and weaknesses of the work.
   - The presenting teacher takes notes.
6. Reflection (5 minutes)
   - The presenting teacher rejoins the discussion and shares what she learned from the feedback, focusing on what was learned rather than defending the work.
   - Responders are silent.
7. Debrief (5 minutes)
   - The facilitator leads an open discussion of the process.
   - The process observer shares what he or she noticed about the way the group functioned.

Standards Protocol

(adapted from a protocol developed by the Center for Collaborative Education)
Purpose: To analyze student work against a specific standard, criteria, or scoring rubric.
Time: approximately 45 minutes.

1. Describe the assignment and the standards that apply (5 minutes)
   - The presenting teacher describes the assignment, discusses which standards the assignment addresses, and outlines the assessment process, rubric, or criteria.
   - The presenting teacher frames a question to focus the discussion.
2. Clarifying questions (5 minutes)
   - Responders ask questions to clarify their understanding.
   - Clarifying questions are factual, straightforward, and nonjudgmental.
   - The presenting teacher answers clarifying questions without going into great detail.
   - Responders take notes.
3. Score the work (5 minutes)
   - Responders individually score the work sample, using the presenting teacher's criteria or rubric.
   - If the presenting teacher failed to bring a rubric, the group can develop one together.
   - The goal is to develop a common idea about the quality of the work.
4. Look at the work (10 minutes)
   - The group discusses discrepancies in the responders' scores while considering questions the work raises in relationship to the standards.
5. Analyze the work (15 minutes)
   - The facilitator asks the presenting teacher to restate the question to confirm the group's focus.
   - The presenting teacher listens as the responders discuss the work and offer feedback.
   - The group is careful to connect their comments to the standards.
6. Reflection (10 minutes)
   - The presenting teacher rejoins the discussion and shares what he learned from the feedback, focusing on what was learned rather than defending the work.
   - Responders are silent.
7. Discuss implications (10 minutes)
   - Both the presenting teacher and responders share new thoughts they have about their teaching practices.

- The group may develop an action plan to further address the issues generated by the discussion.
8. Debrief (5 minutes)
  - Open discussion of the process, led by the facilitator.
  - The process observer shares what he or she noticed about the way the group functioned.

The Consultancy Protocol

(adapted from a protocol developed by the Coalition of Essential Schools, www.essentialschools.org)

Purpose: This protocol is used to allow a group to explore a problem or dilemma.

Time: Approximately 60 minutes.

1. The presenting teacher gives an overview of the issue or dilemma and then poses a focus question. (5 minutes)
2. Responders ask clarifying questions, keeping in mind that they are primarily aimed at helping responders understand the questions and context. The presenter responds to the clarifying questions. (5 minutes)
3. The group asks the presenter probing questions. Probing questions are primarily open ended and are for the responders. These questions should be worded so that they help the presenter clarify and expand her thinking about the issue she has presented. The presenter responds to the probing questions, but there is no discussion by the larger group. (10–15 minutes)
4. Responders discuss the issue or dilemma while the presenting teacher silently takes notes. What did we hear? What didn't we hear that we needed to know more about? What do we think about the question or issue presented? (10–15 minutes)
5. The presenting teacher responds by sharing what she is thinking and the next steps she might take. During this time, the responders listen. (10 minutes)
6. The facilitator opens up the discussion to the whole group. (10 minutes)
7. The process observer leads an open discussion about the process. (5 minutes)

Peeling the Onion: Developing a Problem Protocol

(adapted from Nancy Mohr and the National School Reform Faculty)

Purpose: To provide a structured way to develop an appreciation for the complexity of a problem while avoiding the inclination to start out "solving" it. Most of us are eager to solve problems before we understand their depth. This protocol is designed to help a group peel away the layers to address the deeper issues that lie underneath the surface.

Time: approximately 50 minutes.

1. The presenter explains the dilemma and poses a focus question.
2. Clarifying questions (4 minutes)
3. Round 1: One by one, everyone finishes this statement: "I understand the question to be . . ." The presenter is silent and takes notes.
4. Round 2: One by one, everyone finishes this statement: "One thing I assume to be true about this problem is . . ." The presenter remains silent and takes notes.
5. Round 3: One by one, everyone finishes this statement: "A question this raises for me is . . ." The presenter remains silent and takes notes. If there are more questions among the group, this round may be repeated.
6. Round 4: One by one, everyone poses a question starting with the following: "What if . . . ?" or "Have you thought of . . . ?" The presenter remains silent and takes notes.
7. The presenter reviews notes and says, "Having heard these questions, I think there are implications for . . ."
8. Together, the presenter and responders think of possibilities and options that have surfaced.
9. The process observer leads an open discussion of the process. (5 minutes) Be sure to discuss the following:
   - How was this like peeling an onion?
   - What about the process was useful?
   - Was the process frustrating? If so, how?

A Final Thought

Until we began examining student work, we held on to the shining moments when students such as Jamie showed off their isolated successes as writers. We knew most of our students had a long way to go, but it wasn't until we came together to share ideas and offer feedback that we were able to determine how to move forward. For too long, we had subconsciously insulated ourselves from the constructive feedback that is essential to guided practice. Much like our students, each teacher needed help to know where to go next. We hadn't been challenging ourselves to take risks, and it wasn't until we sat together and asked, "How do you think I could make this student a better writer?" that we were able to move on in our learning.

Part 3

Independence

Anyone involved in professional development will agree that sustaining new learning over the long term can be next to impossible. With changes in leadership, teacher, or instructional programs, the only consistency schools face is change, making sustainability difficult. The last section in this book looks at leadership and how it sustains teacher learners in the independence phase. Chapter 7 focuses on principal leadership, Chapter 8 looks at teacher leadership, and Chapter 9 recognizes the ongoing challenges that never seem to go away.

Principal Leadership

> *What is needed, in a word, is leadership*
> *that creates "constructivist" adult*
> *learning—dialogue and critical inquiry.*
>
> —Tony Wagner

Winter is fast approaching, and the members of the Harrington Book Club let themselves in through the front door, dumping coats and purses on the nearest chair. Carole wears her signature apron and offers us wine as we settle into her cozy kitchen. The fireplace is lighted and the table is set. An hors d'oeuvres platter is within reach, and the chatter is on.

This month we read *Endurance* by Alfred Lansing (1959), the true story of how Ernest Shackleton led his men through the inhospitable region of Antarctica in the early part of the twentieth century. The original plan was to sail to Antarctica and be the first group to cross the continent by foot. But because of worse-than-expected weather, the men were trapped in the frozen ice fields for more than a year. They faced insurmountable barriers, bone-chilling cold, and a lack of food, yet they all survived.

Lisi can never wait until dinner to talk about the book, and this month is no different. "Can you believe what those men went through? I mean, I'm cold tonight and this is nothing. I can't believe they all survived." We talk about human resilience and wonder if we would have the strength to survive if put in the same circumstances. We wonder how these men beat the odds the way they did.

Scholars attribute the survival of the *Endurance* team to Shackleton's leadership, and specifically to his ability to create leaders within the crew. By creating a culture of shared leadership, he was able to put the men in charge of their own fates. He made it clear that they would work together to get out of the dire situation they were in. Shackleton couldn't have done it alone. Nobody could have.

Principals such as Sally also face insurmountable challenges, and they can't do it alone either. With a job description that includes being an instructional leader, gathering resources, managing the budget, offering moral support, increasing test scores, and providing feedback to teachers, principals are pulled in every direction. For their own survival and the survival of their "crew" they must create leaders around them.

On the *Endurance,* Shackleton provided a model of leadership that could serve principals well. When school leaders set out to improve a struggling school, they face tough problems that come with no easy solutions. They need courage to take challenges head-on, no matter how much they fear failure. Leading in adversity isn't easy, yet we can learn much from leaders such as Ernest Shackleton.

First, he teaches us that a leader must *build a crew with diverse talents.* When the time came to hire his crew, Shackleton handpicked his leading crew members from men with whom he had worked on other expeditions. He selected Frank Worsley as captain because he was a talented navigator. Thomas Crean had served in the Irish navy and was a disciplined sailor. Because of Crean's physical power, Shackleton planned to use him as a driver of a sledge team.

When it came time to hire the rest of his crew, Shackleton's interviews were lightning fast and based on appearance and personality. Lansing writes, "When the *Endurance* sailed from England, there could hardly have been a more heterogeneous collection of individuals. They varied from Cambridge University dons to Yorkshire fishermen" (1959). Each man came with his own set of skills. Doctors, artists, scientists, cooks, and carpenters all were ready to risk life and limb for adventure.

Shackleton teaches us that leadership should be *flexible, event specific, and include the whole crew.* He didn't choose his favorites to lead; rather, everyone was given a time and place to take leadership roles. Events changed on a daily basis, and each change presented a new set of demands. Instead of designating himself as an omnipotent leader who handled every situation, Shackleton drew on the talent of each man within his crew. Worsley was the bookish captain, and Crean was a brash Irish sailor with physical strength. They were leaders in different ways at different times.

In elementary schools we often expect teachers to have an impossibly diverse set of skills and knowledge. They are expected to know how to teach math, reading, writing, science, social studies, art, and sometimes, physical education. Many teachers will tell you, "I'm a great math teacher, but I don't feel comfortable teaching writing." Or, "I love teaching social studies, but never get to science." Even beyond knowing their subject matter, teachers must be able to manage student behavior, communicate with parents, and analyze student data. A principal who knows his or her teachers' strengths can tap into their knowledge and expertise when the time is right, thereby disbursing knowledge throughout the faculty.

Shackleton also understood the importance of *allowing leaders to take a break*. On one day, the oldest crew member and carpenter, "Chippy" McNeish, had the necessary skills to shore up the lifeboats. On another, he complained he would prefer to die right there on a snowdrift. Shackleton recognized Chippy for his talents but didn't press him when he wasn't able to contribute. A few teacher leaders cannot shoulder the burden of school change all by themselves. Expecting a few people to be effective teachers while overseeing a school change effort fails to acknowledge that, sooner or later, everyone hits a point of emotional or physical fatigue. Furthermore, the habit of passing on responsibility to a few "chosen ones" sends the message that they are better or smarter in some way than the rest of the teachers. This practice is bad for morale and usually causes other teachers with leadership potential to disengage from the change process.

All members of the *Endurance* crew were reminded to *keep the primary goal in mind*. Survival was the crew's goal, and though most of the men secretly doubted their ability to make it, Shackleton did not permit failure to be a topic for discussion. In a few days, the crew floated hundreds of miles closer to land. Then the currents changed, and they drifted back hundreds more. With every success came an equally heartbreaking failure, yet they inched forward and finally reached land.

Teachers need small successes along the way to give them the energy to keep going. Many of them doubt their efficacy on a daily basis, yet letting these fears surface undermines the momentum that they need to attain a goal.

Finally, Shackleton *encouraged playfulness*. He created joy in the face of despair. As the men waited out the ice they held dogsled races, danced together, and played practical jokes on one another. The stress they were under was enormous, and playfulness helped them stay connected with each other. A sense of humor enabled them to survive and not give up the fight. School principals can encourage playfulness; otherwise the work becomes overwhelming.

Creating an Environment to Encourage and Sustain Teacher Leaders

As we sit around Carole's dinner table discussing Shackleton's leadership, I ask Sally how she creates shared leadership at Harrington. It doesn't take her long to respond: "Like Shackleton, it begins with hiring the right people."

In the beginning, most teachers weren't at Harrington by choice, and a lack of enthusiasm pervaded the school. Sally began making a concerted effort to persuade teacher candidates to *choose* Harrington. In interviews she talked with enthusiasm about her vision for Harrington's future. The message was that this school had potential. One by one, teachers such as Carole began to come on board. In a way these teachers were the pioneers; they wanted to be in a place that made a difference for kids, and Sally made it clear that the place to be was Harrington.

"But the crew isn't enough," she goes on. "I also try to encourage joint decision making."

The creation of a leadership team helped move teachers forward in their thinking. The leadership team started by reading *Schools That Work: Where All Children Read and Write* (Allington and Cunningham 2001), and that research created a common understanding from which to make decisions. No longer was it Sally making the decisions; rather, teachers were in the driver's seat.

"Once the leadership team was up and running, I began planting seeds for other leaders," Sally adds.

Leadership isn't a single person's endeavor; rather, it is part of the greater school culture. An effective principal knows the strengths of his or her teachers, and offers opportunities for leadership at the appropriate time.

Without Carole knowing it, Sally noticed she was teaching poetry in innovative ways. With this in mind, she pulled Carole aside and suggested, "Why don't you start a poetry study group?" Carole liked the idea and recruited me for moral support. Soon enough, our poetry study group was in place. Sally attended every session so she could observe the dynamics of the group and learn how to plant the seeds for the next teacher leader.

With her subtle suggestion, Sally created a new form of professional development while tapping in to Carole's leadership potential. Six years later, study groups are still a regular part of the school culture.

Then Cindy points out, "Sally, you also work hard to establish a shared knowledge base for teachers."

Each year, the school loses a handful of teachers and faces the challenge of replacing them. Whether they stop teaching to start a family, have exciting new prospects in administration or as staff developers, or relocate with their families, there is always teacher turnover.

When facing turnover, Sally knows that establishing a solid base for new teachers is essential. All new teachers receive support from instructional coaches, during grade-level meetings, through observation in labs, in study groups, and throughout professional development sessions. Any new teacher at Harrington will tell you that the first year isn't necessarily easy, but that it is laden with support.

Throughout Alonso's first year, he worked intensively with his instructional coach. In his second year, he observed in Barb Smith's lab classroom. There he saw how what he had been discussing and hearing about looked in a different setting. By then he had a foundation to draw from, and that foundation helped him interact and discuss practice in the lab setting and then take it back to his own classroom. Over time, and as a result of numerous learning opportunities, his foundation became more and more solid.

Sally agrees. "Yes, and I also have to maintain an open definition of a teacher leader, since you never know where leadership will come from."

Sally maintains openness for new ideas, and it is her openness that encourages teachers to volunteer for leadership roles.

She explains: "Recently Alonso asked me if he could start a study group around the book *On Solid Ground* by Sharon Taberski [2000]. He's been reading it in his lab and wanted to share what he has learned with the rest of the faculty. I would have never expected Alonso to come forward like that; he's fairly reserved and is only a second-year teacher. I told him that I think it's a great idea and encouraged him to give it a try." By maintaining openness for new ideas, Sally creates an environment where teachers such as Alonso can feel safe sharing their thinking.

"We also constantly model learning and inquiry," she says. At the core of creating teacher leaders lies the fact that Sally is a learner herself. She participates in every professional study group and grade-level meeting. She sets the tone by challenging herself as a learner, reads professionally, and is a part of every discussion.

"And finally, we have a good time since a sense of humor is needed in our work." She chuckles, takes a sip of wine, and adds, "I guess we are more like the *Endurance* than I thought."

As Sally worked to create a climate of shared leadership, she admits, she didn't always know where things were headed. Her conviction that every decision had to be based on the best interests of the students helped her define the school's future. She made sure the conversations were grounded in instruction, and as time passed, the vision was defined. It was then that the teacher leaders began to reveal themselves.

Inquiry Stance

Linda Lambert suggests that to encourage shared leadership schools should "[d]evelop a culture of inquiry that includes a continuous cycle of reflecting, questioning, gathering evidence, and planning improvement" (1998). In a culture of inquiry and shared leadership, there are no predetermined answers or outcomes. Instead, and like Lambert suggests, a complex dilemma is considered over the long term. Questions lead to sources of information and evidence, which in turn leads to the planning of next steps.

Consider an example. When I arrived at Harrington, there was no rhyme or reason around reading instruction. Little discussion took place, and there were teachers doing everything from drilling with worksheets, to using outdated basal reading series, to subscribing to a whole-language approach in which students read a lot but with little instruction. Sally's thoughts about reading instruction began to change when Ellin Keene shared her new thinking about reading comprehension at a Public Education & Business Coalition leadership seminar in the Harrington library. Ellin told a group of principals and teachers about the strategies readers use to comprehend text and shared the latest research on the subject. As she reflected on the current state of reading instruction, Sally knew this was an exciting area to be explored.

Shortly thereafter, the whole school embarked on an exploration of reading comprehension strategies. We read articles together and Marjory modeled how reading comprehension instruction looked in the classroom. Slowly we developed a common language that included new terms such as *schema, metacognition,* and *synthesis.* We were thinking about reading in new ways, and we were learning together.

Our learning didn't happen in a straight line. We didn't simply read about these strategies and then perfectly adapt them to the classroom. Rather, the process was recursive, and gradually our understanding of the comprehension strategies deepened. But throughout it all, we maintained an inquiry stance. We used questions to expand our thinking. We fought the tendency to box ourselves in to one definition of comprehension instruction, and instead reveled in the process of defining it for ourselves.

One Focus at a Time

Schools, especially low-performing schools, can become a black hole of initiatives and reforms. Grants with different promised outcomes, district expectations, parent involvement programs, and student interventions create an atmosphere where everything is happening and nothing gets done. Some principals may think they don't have the luxury to pick and choose between the issues that need their focus and attention—after all, there are so many needs. Because of the fragmentation of purpose and objective, being a successful leader in these settings can be nearly impossible.

To maintain a single focus, keep instruction at the epicenter, and even more specifically, choose one area of instruction as the professional development focus. Rather than subscribing to global goals such as, "We will make our students lifelong learners," or "We will raise student achievement," narrow it down. For example, decide "Our goal is to make our students better writers," or "We will build our students' background knowledge and oral language," then focus professional development activities around that single goal. Once a specific goal has been determined, think broadly about how to accomplish it.

Setting specific goals can also be directly linked to accountability measures. For example, when Harrington students did poorly on the state writing assessment, we realized our work in writing wasn't taking our students far enough, so teaching writing became the professional development focus for the entire school year.

We began by giving each teacher an empty three-ring binder. It was empty because we would define our thinking about teaching writing together.

Next we read *Teaching Writing: Balancing Process and Product* by Gail E. Tompkins (1994). As we read and discussed what we believed, the scope of our charge came into view. Tompkins helped us realize that we had the process of writer's workshop well established, but that we knew little about the domains of writing. We found her chapter on expository writing particularly useful and started there.

At this point, Marjory decided to nudge our thinking. She suggested we compare our students' writing with benchmark papers from outside the school. She knew we had no idea what a proficient piece of writing looked like, and thought we had better find out. (For more on this see Chapter 6.)

After we had spent a few months analyzing our students' writing against the benchmark papers, a teacher suggested we do the same thing with the parents. We thought it was a brilliant suggestion, so at our next Family Night we invited parents into their child's classroom. There, the teacher explained the school's focus on teaching writing and passed out anonymous sample papers, benchmark papers, and a writing rubric. With help from the teacher, the parents used the rubric and benchmarks to score the sample papers. Inevitably the parents asked, "How does my son or daughter's writing compare?" The teachers were ready with folders of the children's writing, and it didn't take long for the parents to understand how their child measured against the content standards. Like teachers, the parents needed a point of comparison to truly understand how their son or daughter was doing. It wasn't until we spent the whole year focusing on learning about how to better teach writing that we were able to understand the differences ourselves.

During this time, our professional development included many layers. Not only did we take the time to examine student writing in grade-level teams, but we also discussed writing with the whole staff, worked with our instructional coaches individually on writing, and brought our new learning to the parents of our students.

Practical Steps

For teachers to feel comfortable taking leadership roles, they have to have a broad scope of professional development options. One teacher may feel comfortable leading a study group, whereas others may prefer observing colleagues. Just as a salad is better with more ingredients, so is professional development. The following professional development options create opportunities for teacher leaders:

1. *Reading with colleagues.* Reading is an ongoing piece of professional development. The expectation is for teachers to read both literature and professional books and articles.

2. *Discussing the big ideas.* Dialogue is essential to the development of shared leadership. Time for professional dialogue is embedded into the school day. Grade-level or team meetings are the norm so teachers can discuss successes and struggles, examine student work, and share plans for the future.

3. *Reflecting on a regular basis.* Reflecting on student growth is an important way to determine the next steps in instruction. Reflection can be useful when considering new ideas or strategies to use with students and better ways to organize learning time, and to share the successes and challenges we face as teachers.

4. *Observing colleagues.* Teachers are given the opportunity to observe and reflect on the practices of other teachers. By setting up a lab model within a school, organizing release time for teachers to visit other schools, or using videotapes of model teachers working with students, teachers are no longer isolated. (For more on the lab model and observation, see Chapter 3.)

5. *Collaborative planning.* Teacher isolation is the primary cause of stagnation and lack of growth within a school community. The structures for collaborative planning are necessary to achieve a unified vision and shared leadership. During collaborative planning sessions, teachers bring varied and diverse strengths and perspectives.

6. *Differentiated learning.* Just like a classroom of children, no teacher draws from the same set of experiences. Teachers need diverse opportunities for professional development that are geared toward meeting them where they are and carrying them forward.

The Socratic Seminar as a Tool for Discussion

Creating an environment of shared leadership depends on including all stakeholders in the decision-making process. Socratic seminar is a useful tool for encouraging open-ended discussion and comes from the great philosopher's belief that the process of dialogue forces participants to clarify their ideas. Socrates played the role of facilitator and even feigned ignorance to encourage others to construct their own knowledge about a given subject. Here's how a school might use the Socratic seminar to create shared leadership:

1. *A compelling text.* The Socratic seminar is based upon a shared reading, preferably one that raises important questions. The leader asks participants to read the text beforehand and take careful notes, such as questions, what it reminded them of, or how it connects to their practice.
2. *A guiding question.* The leader opens the discussion with a provocative question and invites participants to begin responding. Participants continue responding until the leader calls time. Enough time is allocated so that the discussion takes a slow and thoughtful pace.
3. *A neutral leader.* The leader probes participants' thinking by asking questions when the group seems to need direction. The leader keeps the group engaged in the text while allowing participants time to construct new ideas.
4. *An open-ended discussion.* Many times, a Socratic seminar leaves a group with more questions than answers, yet helps define a deeper, and shared, understanding of the issue at hand.

Guidelines for a Socratic Seminar The quality of a Socratic seminar depends on the preparation of the participants as well as their ability to listen actively and share their ideas and questions. Share the following guidelines with participants:

1. participants sit in a circle, so everyone can be seen and heard;
2. comments make specific reference to the text;
3. participants actively listen to each other;
4. participants refrain from speaking until another person's thought has been finished;
5. Socratic seminar is not a debate. If the conversation stays between a few participants, the leader must pull in ideas from other participants;
6. participants may pass;
7. participants can be encouraged to write reflectively during the discussion;
8. participants shouldn't stay confused, and should ask for clarification;
9. participants discuss ideas related to the text instead of opinions;
10. participants talk to each other and not just the leader; and
11. a debriefing period allows everyone to hear how the participants felt about the discussion and process.

A Final Thought

Reaching independence on the gradual release continuum depends upon creating a belief system about learning, and that very belief system encourages shared leadership. Though teachers move through the gradual release continuum repeatedly and in different ways, the goal is for them to become independent or highly proficient in certain aspects of their teaching. It could be Sue's work with teaching English Language Acquisition or perhaps Keith's depth of knowledge about small-group instruction. Learning is about passion, and it's okay for Sue and Keith to become proficient in different areas. The key is for their leader to encourage such learning and inquiry, and then tap in to that knowledge when the time is right.

Much like the constructivist approach to teaching is designed to encourage children to be reflective and passionate learners, the constructivist approach to teacher leadership has the same outcome. Leadership is not a burden for a few to shoulder; it is something to be shared throughout a school. It took awhile for Harrington to become a safe place where teachers felt comfortable taking risks, and that comfort is the essence of a learning community. If Ernest Shackleton hadn't been able to draw from the strengths of his entire crew, they probably wouldn't have survived. Shackleton was the primary leader, just like a principal is the primary leader in a school. But it's that leader's capacity to create leaders among the crew that makes the difference.

Chapter 8

Teacher Leadership:
Switching Roles

*Only those who dare to fail greatly can
ever achieve greatly.*

—Robert F. Kennedy

I take a quick look around the conference room and wonder if a mistake has been made. Am I supposed to be here? Why on earth have I been invited to this gathering of teacher leaders?

Introductions circle the group and a knot develops in my stomach. "I had better come up with something intelligent to say or they might be on to me," I think. I glance over at Carole to see the same worried expression on her face. In just a few moments, it is apparent that the teachers around us think deeply about their practice, are well read in terms of the research, and are innovative when it comes to both instruction and how their schools operate. They don't settle for the status quo that is so readily provided by the educational establishment and are always searching for better ways to meet the students' needs. Together, our group will participate in the Capacity Building Initiative (CBI), a training-for-trainers program that encourages teacher leadership. As we listen to the others, we are relieved to hear the same refrain: "I'm not sure what I have to offer a group like this, but I am here to learn as much as I can." Nobody seems to know how he or she will define his or her new leadership role. What do we have to offer? Where are we most comfortable? We are learners ready to struggle with the challenges in our schools, yet no teacher in the room is ready to admit to being a teacher leader. Maybe that will come with time.

Teacher Leaders Sustain Professional Development

Most teachers have experienced professional development efforts that start strong only to run out of steam. A consultant comes in to work with a school faculty for days, weeks, or years, and sooner or later the "expert" wraps up, leaving the teachers on their own. Schools intend to sustain the work, but too often it goes down in the teachers' memories as another fly-by-night initiative.

Maintaining a professional learning community is tough because principal and teacher turnover can wipe the slate clean. Not to mention the fact that many school districts change their focus as predictably as the seasons change. As Harrington worked toward becoming a learning community, it spent years in the first two stages of the gradual release continuum. In fact, modeling and guided practice will always be a large part of Harrington's professional development model. But as more knowledge was acquired, school structures began to change and teacher leaders began to carry the effort toward independence.

All new learning begins with modeling, is supported through guided practice, and is sustained through new thinking and permanent changes in behavior. When I learned to garden in Colorado, I read books about plants that grow well in our dry climate. I regularly cornered experts at my local nursery so I could get my questions answered. I made mistakes and ended up with a few plant casualties, but whenever I got into trouble, I knew where to find help. I've moved beyond needing all the support I needed then, and now I view myself as a fairly proficient gardener. Sure, I need some advice now and then, but I have made it to independence. The same goes for professional development. If learning is taken all the way to the independence stage, new learning becomes ingrained in the school culture and the efforts are not only sustained but continue to flourish.

Training Teacher Leaders

Although teachers are quite comfortable working with children, leadership requires an entirely different set of skills. When the best teachers are plucked from the classroom to become instructional leaders among their peers, they rarely receive any guidance about how to work with other adults. Teacher leaders need to be trained in strategies for working with adult learners. They need a repertoire of facilitation frameworks (see "Practical Steps"), protocols for leading adults in discussion, and even the most basic information about how to organize their time in a new role.

The Public Education & Business Coalition designed the Capacity Building Initiative to offer this much-needed support to teachers who have decided to venture beyond the comfortable boundaries of classroom teaching. The credit for the development of CBI goes to Ellin Keene, Kristin Venable, Colleen Buddy, and Chryse Hutchins. When schools enter their final year of professional development, two teacher leaders participate in CBI. Together these teachers learn how to function as leaders in their schools by attending seminars, observing staff developers, and reading professionally. The schools benefit from this training because their teachers develop a deeper understanding of adult learning and formulate a plan for leading new learning in their schools.

CBI is built upon the principle of scholarly study because teacher leaders must know and understand the research. Participants are involved in regular discussions of professional readings focused on the content areas, leadership, and school change. They are expected to be reflective and to come to discussions with more questions than answers.

As we know from the gradual release continuum, modeling and observation are critical elements in the early stages of learning. Therefore CBI participants are also given the opportunity to observe many different adult learning scenarios, such as the instruction and facilitation that takes place during a lab, a staff developer providing professional development for other teachers, or a facilitator working with a school faculty to negotiate a large-scale school reform effort.

Switching Roles

I vividly remember my first CBI meeting in the fall of 1997, and now I am the person at the door greeting teachers as they enter the room. This year, Carole's daughter Lisi participates. Lisi is a first- and second-grade teacher at Harrington. She recently decided that she might have something to offer beyond her expertise as a teacher, and she thinks she is ready for a new challenge. The cohort also includes Susan Levy, another first- and second-grade teacher at Harrington. Susan and I worked closely as teacher and coach, and from that experience she decided she would like to offer other teachers the kind of support I offered her. Along with Susan and Lisi are teachers from many other schools involved in professional development. From this experience, the teachers will be encouraged to open up their classrooms for colleagues to observe their instruction. They may opt to become an instructional coach. (For more on this, see Chapter 4.) Some could choose to organize classes for other teachers on issues such as working with parents and teaching second-language learners. Perhaps they will lead study groups or Critical Friends Groups in their school.

After walking in their shoes, I know that viewing oneself as a teacher leader can be intimidating, so I start the meeting by asking, "What worries you the

89

most about taking on the role of teacher leader?" Groups of four begin to list their greatest fears, and after several minutes we share their questions and doubts.

1. Am I ready to do this?
2. Will I be alienated if I take a leadership role?
3. What about reluctant adults?
4. How will I scaffold my colleagues' needs?
5. How do I find a balance between being vague and being prescriptive?
6. What kinds of expertise do I need?
7. Do I have enough time to take on a new role?
8. Are my communication skills up to par?
9. Will others scrutinize me?
10. Is my professional vocabulary adequate?
11. Will I be considered a prophet-in-my-own-land?
12. Will I be able to motivate other adult learners?
13. Will I be pulled away from my students?

The doubts listed in our first CBI meeting are no surprise. Teachers are more comfortable working with children than with adults, and the difference between the two is vast, making switching roles difficult. Furthermore, teachers have a lot on their plate, and they may feel that being asked to contribute as teacher leaders is too much. Because a teacher is measured solely by student achievement, many with leadership potential are closing their classroom doors to hunker down to the task at hand.

The problem is that if every teacher takes this viewpoint, any hope for sustaining school change will be brought to a standstill. In earlier chapters, I explained how collaboration, observation, shared study, and instructional coaching create a shared instructional vision and offer the guided practice that is necessary for teacher learning. I also said that improving a school's performance is dependent upon building a collaborative school community. Therefore, there is no room for hunkering down and refusing to take on leadership roles. In any effort to change, it isn't enough to stop at the guided-practice phase. Independence must be reached or the effort will be all for naught, and in more than any other phase, reaching independence depends upon teacher leadership.

When Carole and I were figuring out how to lead change efforts at Harrington, Carole decided she was more comfortable opening her classroom to observing teachers. Her classroom would be her medium for sharing her thinking, and the last thing she wanted was to work under the constraints of an unknown classroom and with unknown children. Each year, Carole hosts visitors from other schools in the Denver area as well as many others from across the country. She has never believed she has good teaching all figured out, but instead claims that opening her classroom to other teachers has given her the opportunity to reflect on her teaching, making her a better teacher every time a visitor crosses her threshold.

Carole also serves as a teacher leader for the other Harrington teachers. She hosts the Harrington Book Club, facilitates study groups, orders most of the children's literature that supplies the school, and spends endless amounts of time supporting new teachers with the ideas and resources they need. As a leader, Carole never hesitates to stand true to her beliefs about what is best for Harrington students and as a result is a pillar of support for the entire Harrington faculty.

For me, the distance between a teacher observing in a lab classroom and implementing what they saw seemed vast, so I decided to work alongside teachers in their own classrooms as an instructional coach. In this role, I had the opportunity to support Harrington teachers in their classrooms through demonstration lessons, coteaching, individual planning, and grade-level planning. It was a big leap from my own classroom to the classrooms of others, and even with training, switching roles proved difficult.

When I started teaching teachers rather than students, I had to be ready to be in the public eye. It was quite a transition to move from the private environment of my classroom to the public world of a staff developer. In my new role, I regularly modeled effective instructional strategies for other teachers. There were frequent conversations about instruction, and I had to be confident that I had the knowledge to address the issues they raised. I also had to be more comfortable seeking out information, another public act. Rather than fear asking a dumb question, I had no choice but to learn from my colleagues. This environment of publicly giving and receiving information took some getting used to.

Stimulating other people's thinking was also new to me. Sure, I did it all the time with kids, but it felt different with adults, as if my knowledge would be judged. Teacher leaders walk a fine line between giving teachers ideas and prodding their thinking. My goal was to empower teachers to reflect upon their practice and to resist merely giving them a lesson idea for the next day. At the same time, I understood that there is a practical level to what we do, and that teachers must feel they are learning both ideas and theory. Early on, I found it difficult to get teachers to reflect on shared learning experiences. I worried that if I didn't give them concrete ideas, they would doubt my effectiveness. With time, though, I became more comfortable asking probing questions of teachers to push their own thinking.

I was also intimidated by feeling that I had to be an expert at everything. Now I realize my job really was about facilitating teachers' thinking.

Although I needed a substantial knowledge base to draw from, I found the task less daunting when I considered myself a partner rather than an expert. When working with teachers, I now take the stance that I am there to help them think through whatever challenges they are facing. More important, this approach makes teachers more comfortable, because their ideas and experiences are valued.

It helped me to specialize and refine my work with literacy instruction. My role was limited to supporting literacy, so I was able to focus my learning on literacy alone. I read books and professional journals, kept an eye out for articles that addressed my specific subject area, and talked a lot with other teachers and staff developers about what was working for them in teaching reading and writing. If my focus had been too broad, I would have had less time to develop a depth of expertise. Specialization helped me build my confidence and skills as a staff developer.

I had to be passionate and open minded. Balancing what others were doing while staying flexible were both important. I had to be passionate while honoring the work of others.

Finally, when switching roles, I found that having partners made an enormous difference. I was one of three specialists at Harrington, and we worked together constantly. The other specialists helped me through challenges and offered me a support system. On difficult days we would troubleshoot what to do next. On successful days, we celebrated together. Working with colleagues made a difficult job more rewarding.

Switching roles brought me back to apprenticeship all over again. Luckily I got the support I needed to do the work, and with that support I became an empowered and passionate teacher leader.

Practical Steps

What is the content of our training-for-trainers program?

In CBI, the focus is on adult learning and our seminars include the following topics:

- Effective professional development. Teachers hear from experienced staff developers about the challenges they face when working with teachers as well as the lessons they have learned along the way. They also share how they structure their work with teachers for the most benefit.
- Change theories. Teachers read and discuss *Who Moved My Cheese?* by Spencer Johnson (1998) and *Transitions: Strategies for Coping with the*

Difficult, Painful, and Confusing Times in Your Life by William Bridges (1980) to learn more about how change affects our day-to-day lives as teachers and people.

- Learning trends by generation. Teachers look at the research by Honey and Mumford (1982) and hear from an expert in this field of study.
- The gradual release for adult learners. Teachers discuss how learning among adults compares with learning among children, using the gradual release continuum as our frame of reference. To do this, we reflect upon a time we learned something new so we can understand the stages every learner moves through.
- Facilitation frameworks. Teachers learn various frameworks to facilitate discussions among teachers (see below).
- Protocols for working with adults. Teachers experience various protocols for Critical Friends Groups and text-based discussions such as study groups or book clubs (see Chapters 2 and 6).
- Planning our future work. Teachers spend time planning the work they hope to accomplish in their schools, using the questions in "Planning Next Steps."

Dynamics of Facilitation (C2P3)

(adapted from Buddy)
The following facilitation protocol is a useful tool for ensuring that all the necessary aspects of facilitation are in place. When leading a group, use the C2P3 as concrete steps along the way.

1. *Content.* What is it? Are you facilitating a study group, a grade-level planning session, a debriefing? Is your focus reading, writing, or another content area? What background should you know before beginning the discussion?
2. *Context.* What is the big picture? What are the issues or needs for this particular group of teachers? Are there barriers for implementation? If so, what are they? How soon should the work be implemented and how in-depth should it be?
3. *People.* Who will be affected, supported, challenged? Who may have doubts about impending change? Are you leaving anyone out of the discussion? How will you ensure that everyone's voice will be heard?
4. *Process.* How will the change happen? What are the steps for implementation? How will the teachers know they are on the right track? Will there be benchmarks along the way?

5. *Purpose.* Why is this change necessary and/or important? How will it meet the needs of the people who are being affected? How will teachers be sure their self-interests will be met in the process?

A Facilitation Framework

(adapted from Buddy)
Another tool to organize facilitation, the following framework takes you through the facilitation process.

1. Getting started
   - Set norms. Decide how the group would like to work together.
   - Frame the task. Outline what the group is there to discuss.
   - Outline the process. Detail how the time together will be organized.
2. Moving along
   - Maintain focus. Keep the group on task and if necessary revisit the earlier "frame the task" discussion.
   - Listen to what is said and make connections. It can be challenging to hear what people are saying. Try to listen carefully, avoid making assumptions, and make connections to other aspects of the conversation.
   - Direct and manage energy. Give the group breaks, snacks, and anything else they need to keep going.
   - Invite participation. In a nonthreatening manner, invite the more quiet teachers to participate. Break into small groups and pairs to encourage the less vocal teachers to talk with colleagues.
   - Manage time and transitions. Negotiate transitions with the group. They will most likely have a preference for breaks, how much time is spent on a certain subject, and any other time issues that arise.
   - Direct the process. Direct the process while staying neutral. Facilitation is more about getting the participants to come to their own conclusions than you telling them what those conclusions should be.
   - Legitimize all perspectives. Honor all teachers in the room, even those with a different perspective.
   - Determine recording and documentation. Keep notes from the process. If there are more meetings, recap the notes from the previous session so the same information isn't rehashed. If teachers are absent, determine how they will stay informed.
3. Wrapping up
   - Synthesize. Pull together a short statement to sum up what transpired.

Outside facilitators may have an easier time doing this because they are less mired in the conversation.

- Determine next steps. Lead the group to determine how they will proceed from here. Be explicit about the next steps and determine who will be responsible for seeing those promises through.
- Evaluate. Ask the group to evaluate the day's progress. Was the time useful? If not, what should be changed?

Planning Next Steps

When planning your work as a teacher leader, do you see yourself

- facilitating study groups?
- inviting teachers into your classroom to observe your instruction?
- implementing and publishing a research project?
- coteaching with other teachers in your school?
- forming Critical Friends Groups in your school?
- modeling instruction for the teachers in your school?
- serving on a leadership team?
- serving in an advisory capacity at the district level?
- presenting at conferences or workshops?

Have you thought about the degree to which you want your work to focus on

- teachers at or around your grade level?
- new teachers in your school?
- teachers throughout your whole school?
- parents in your school?
- paraprofessionals in your school?
- teachers, parents, or paraprofessionals in other schools?

What are your particular areas of comfort relative to teaching and learning?

- teaching in certain content areas such as reading, writing, math, social studies, science;
- classroom management;
- classroom environment and organization;
- conferring;

- flexible grouping strategies;
- effective assessment strategies;
- integrating the curriculum;
- implementation of standards;
- children's literature.

A Final Thought

For Carole and me, the job of leading change wasn't easy. There were many reasons to close our classroom doors and carry on alone. After all, isn't leading change an energy drain? Don't our students provide us with enough challenges? Wouldn't it be better to improve our teaching for the sake of our students? We learned that the opposite is true. Switching roles, challenging ourselves, and working collaboratively gave us energy rather than taking it away. We each discovered our own place where we could contribute to the school as a whole while still supporting individual students.

Today, Carole and I support the next generation of teacher leaders. With their CBI training completed, both Lisi and Susan have decided to take positions as literacy coaches at Harrington. Through their leadership, who knows how many leaders will follow? If I sat in that conference room on the first day of CBI training all over again, I would introduce myself much differently. "Hi, my name is Diane, and I'm a teacher leader."

Chapter

Finding the Courage to Get There

There is no road so smooth that it has
no rough spots.

—Panamanian Proverb

I t's 4:30 in the morning when my friends pick me up. I throw my backpack and hiking boots into the back of their Jeep and we drive west. Colorado has fifty-five peaks that are 14,000 feet or higher, and today we will climb two of them. Luckily I am with my friend Tom, who has climbed every fourteener in the state of Colorado, and he will be my coach. We arrive at the trailhead, pull out our gear, lace up our boots, and head toward the summit. "This isn't so bad," I think as we hike through mountain meadows blanketed with Colorado wildflowers. Then the climb gets steeper, and we encounter a layer of scree, medium-size volcanic rock that sits one on top of the other like a house of cards. We must be careful when hiking through scree because with each step, the rocks shift beneath us, the surface is unsteady, and the drop is dramatic.

In Harrington's quest to improve student achievement, we have been climbing through scree for a long time now. Every step has resulted in a loss of footing. We have walked carefully and moved uphill ever so slowly. We have taken only a moment to look at the peak looming above, because even a glimpse reminds us of the terrain we still have to cover. Some may never make it to the summit; the weather may turn or they may not have the strength to go on. Instead they will turn back. Everyone knows that being atop a mountain is dangerous, so why not retreat to safer footing? The reason is the children. We know they are capable and need help showing it. We know they want to succeed in spite of the daily burdens of poverty, such as not having a winter coat in the middle of January, having parents they never see because of long hours at work, fear of deportation, and many other factors we can't even begin to understand. Although we can't control poverty, we can control the school environment in which these children spend time every day. We can provide a rigorous yet supportive school experience; we can provide coats, breakfast, and other necessities; and most important, we can let these children know we care about them. This desire doesn't come from a state mandate; it comes from caring about children. The teachers who continue to struggle up the scree know the importance of their work.

At Harrington, the approach has been to prepare the teachers for the climb by offering them many modes of learning and support. Some teachers need the early support that the gradual release continuum provides so they are given opportunities to observe exemplary instruction, discuss practice, and receive feedback. Others have more experience on the mountainside and require a different kind of support. Perhaps they take leadership roles to support the others, or receive more refined feedback on their practice. No two climbers are alike, and our professional development structure supports these differences.

This book outlines many careful steps we took as we worked our way through the scree. Never has our footing been easy. And never has the summit seemed close enough to reach. But it's there, that much we know for sure.

Teacher Turnover

Every year Sally faces teacher turnover, because the day-to-day challenges of working in a high-poverty school never let up. Many teachers commit their heart and soul, only to burn out and become disillusioned. Others choose new paths in life and can't remain at the school for personal reasons. Paul decides to move to San Diego for a fresh start. Ligia has a baby. Alyssa is admitted to Harvard's School of Education. Each of these teachers, and every other one who has left the school, had a powerful presence within the school community and is a major loss. Paul always challenged our thinking, Alyssa was a calming presence, and Ligia was one of our few instructional coaches who spoke fluent Spanish. Each teacher who moves on leaves a void. Sure, Sally has hired good teachers to replace them, but constantly integrating new teachers into the school community takes time and energy.

Changes in District Leadership

Another factor that makes the peak seem outside of our reach is changes in district leadership. When I climbed fourteeners, I had Tom to coach me and support me through my struggles. He was my leader. Yet our school district has failed to offer any consistent support for the climbers in our school. In the eight years I spent in the district, I worked for five superintendents, an average of one per 1.6 years. With such frequent changes in leadership comes a continual change of focus. We got used to "riding out" district-led reforms, because they rarely seemed to address the issues we faced in the schools. Why would anyone become invested in something that is destined to change?

Student Mobility

I notice Mayra is absent for the third day in a row. "Has anyone seen Mayra?" I ask. "She has been absent since Monday."

Miguel says, "Miss, I think she went to Mexico."

"Yeah," Tony says, "they moved."

I sigh. Mayra has been in my class for only a few months. She arrived from Mexico in October, and now it's the middle of January and she's disappeared. For the first month she hardly uttered a word in Spanish or English, and she finally was beginning to join in with the other students. I glance over at her desk and think, "Another one gone without even a good-bye."

At my break, I carefully take Mayra's pencils, crayons, spiral notebooks, and loose papers out of her desk. I pack them into a grocery bag and add it to the bags I've saved from other students who have left without any warning. There's a chance Mayra will come back, and if she does, I'd at least like to return her things.

Not only does the superintendent change on a regular basis, but so does Harrington's student population. In a fifth-grade classroom, an average of only five out of twenty-five students have been at Harrington since kindergarten. In one year alone, I received nine new students in the first two weeks of January. Not only is it heartbreaking to work with students such as Mayra for three months, only to never see them again, but it makes getting our students to the summit quite a challenge. How can we be held accountable when many of our students have been in our classroom for only a few days or weeks leading up to the state test in February?

Bad Press

Nobody forced me to climb those fourteeners. I wasn't up there because I had been goaded, threatened, or coerced into it. I was up there because I wanted to be there. Lately, the approach to improve our public schools has been through threats and intimidation. We hear that if we don't improve our test scores, our school will be taken over by the state. I'm not sure where the motivation lies in this approach, and I know, after being on the receiving end, that these threats don't make us continue to inch up that mountain. We are perched at 13,000 feet because we want to be, and we stay there because we are encouraged. Tom tells me, "Don't worry, Diane. Just go slowly and you'll make it." He never makes me doubt that I can do it, and as a result, I never do.

This morning the front page of the *Denver Post* reads, "Complete School-by-School CSAP Scores on Pages 18–19A." Of course I turn straight to the tables to see how schools did on the state reading test. Last week Sally explained that most of Harrington's third graders tested in English for the first time. She was worried about the results because many of the students weren't yet proficient English speakers. As I find the Harrington scores, I'm not surprised to see that they dropped a few percentage points since last year. I understand why students' scores have declined, but the newspaper on my breakfast table doesn't tell this side of the story. It simply shows a series of numbers and leaves it up to the public to draw their own conclusions. The challenge of improving student achievement is complex and wrought with barriers to success, and test scores oversimplify what is happening at a school such as Harrington.

Schools are called "failing" and principals such as Sally struggle to keep their teachers motivated in the face of failure. The underlying assumption is that teachers are sitting around and not working as hard as they can. If they really cared, wouldn't their students begin to achieve at alarming rates? The truth is that most of the teachers do care; otherwise they wouldn't have kept up the climb.

Approaching the Summit

In light of all the challenges Harrington has faced, there have been many successes along the way. No longer does Harrington have trouble filling positions. Word has gotten around that it supports teacher learning, and teachers want to come on board in spite of the enormous challenges they will face. The learning community that we worked so hard to create continues to support Sally's determined climbers.

Thanks to a focus on professional development, teachers at Harrington are better trained. They know the research behind teaching children to read and write, and most important, they know how to put that research into practice. The philosophy at Harrington is well defined and well articulated. Yet in spite of all we've become, learning never ceases. We've moved through the gradual release continuum more times than anyone can count, and we will move through many more times in the future. We left the trailhead to begin climbing up the mountain years ago, and we are still somewhere beneath the summit. We ask ourselves why we ever decided to do this in the first place, when it would be so much easier to turn back and say it was just too darn hard. The answer is simple: it's the children. Someday they will stand on that mountaintop with us, that much we know.

A Final Note

To those of us in the middle of it all, the change process at Harrington seemed to come from a planetary alignment rather than anything special we had done. After all, we became learners in the effort to better meet the needs of our students. Isn't that true at every school and for every teacher?

In retrospect, the involvement of the Public Education & Business Coalition (PEBC) is what began to change our thinking regarding teacher learning. As a nonprofit organization supporting schools and teacher quality in the Denver metro area since 1983, the PEBC has been an unending source of current research and practice in the areas of reading, writing, information literacy, and mathematics. With this support, the PEBC pushed us to reflect upon our practice, encouraged us to have conversations about our teaching, and modeled exemplary instruction so we could begin to understand where our learning was headed.

Your reasons for heading down this path may be different from ours, and your support system probably will be different as well. I hope this book will encourage you to be creative when you rethink how your school offers professional development. Good luck to you all.

Some of Our Favorite Books and Videos for Study Groups

Literacy—Reading and Writing

Build a Literate Classroom by Donald H. Graves
This resource is designed to help teachers rethink learning to improve their literacy instruction. Included are Graves's signature "Actions," which are designed to make the book practical for classroom application.

Classrooms That Work: They Can All Read and Write by Richard Allington and Patricia M. Cunningham
This book offers a comprehensive look at how classrooms can be reorganized to offer better literacy instruction. It offers the reader concrete ideas that include recommendations, such as the following: children need to read a lot, children need to read at their level, children need to read a wide variety of materials, and children need to be taught to comprehend what they read.

In the Company of Children by Joanne Hindley
Hindley shares experiences from her third-grade classroom at the Manhattan New School. It is written in a conversational style, as if the reader were observing the author in action. The reader takes away both thoughtful and practical ideas for implementing reading/writing workshops.

Lifetime Guarantees: Towards Ambitious Literacy Teaching
by Shelley Harwayne
Harwayne describes her overall beliefs about literacy instruction by focusing on each aspect that she thinks teachers need to consider. This book is full of colorful anecdotes that both enlighten and inspire the reader.

What Really Matters for Struggling Readers: Designing Research-Based Programs by Richard L. Allington
In this book, Allington suggests four key considerations for supporting struggling readers: time to practice reading, reading books at their reading level, learning to read fluently, and developing thoughtful literacy.

Writing

A Writer's Notebook: Unlocking the Writer Within You by Ralph Fletcher
In this useful tool for students and teachers alike, Fletcher takes the mystery out of writing. The reader learns ideas for recording thoughts and observations, as writers do.

Craft Lessons: Teaching Writing K–8 by Ralph Fletcher and Joann Portalupi
A follow-up to *What a Writer Needs* (following), *Craft Lessons* gives concrete examples for authentic writing instruction.

For the Good of the Earth and the Sun: Teaching Poetry by Georgia Heard
The author shares her experiences as both a writer and teacher of poetry. She includes a rich collection of poetry that brings to life the nuances of the form as well as concrete suggestions for teaching poetry to students of all ages.

Lessons from a Child: On the Teaching and Learning of Writing by Lucy Calkins
One of Calkins's earliest books on the writing process, this one tells the story of one child's growth in writing while offering examples of the reading conferences and mini-lessons that propelled her learning.

What a Writer Needs by Ralph Fletcher
Fletcher shares his experience as a writer, and offers strategies for extending student writing. Each chapter focuses on a different aspect of high-quality writing, such as voice, dialogue, and description. Fletcher also shares examples of children's writing.

Reading

Better than Life by Daniel Pennac
A best-seller in France, and now translated into English, *Better than Life* gives Pennac the chance to share the joys of reading, including his *Reader's Bill of Rights*.

I Read It, but I Don't Get It: Comprehension Strategies for Adolescent Readers
by Cris Tovani
Many high school students are challenged by comprehending text. In this book, Cris Tovani uses humor and stories from her classroom to share how she teaches comprehension strategies in her high school classroom.

Listening In: Children Talk About Books (and Other Things)
by Thomas Newkirk
Listen to children as they read and discuss books. Newkirk makes children's learning public and describes how they create their own understanding.

Mosaic of Thought: Teaching Comprehension in a Reader's Workshop
by Ellin Oliver Keene and Susan Zimmermann
A theoretical look at reading comprehension strategies, this book discusses each strategy through the eyes of the adult reader.

Nonfiction Matters: Reading, Writing, and Research in Grades 3–8
by Stephanie Harvey
A resource for teachers interested in combining reading, writing, and research in third- through eighth-grade classrooms. Filled with real-life examples of student work and teaching ideas, this book leaves the reader knowing exactly what to do next.

On Solid Ground: Strategies for Teaching Reading K–3 by Sharon Taberski
In this practical and research-based book, Taberski shares her reading instruction at the Manhattan New School. *On Solid Ground* offers not only a strong rationale for her literacy instruction but also many examples of student work and reproducibles for teachers interested in trying her techniques.

Reading with Meaning: Teaching Comprehension in the Primary Grades
by Debbie Miller
Miller opens the doors to her classroom and welcomes the reader to spend the school year with her first graders. Organized chronologically, beginning in September, this book describes how she teaches reading comprehension strategies. Included are her beliefs about teaching young students to read along with many real-life examples of student thinking.

Strategies That Work: Teaching Comprehension to Enhance Understanding
by Stephanie Harvey and Anne Goudvis
The practical companion to *Mosaic of Thought,* this book discusses the theory

behind the reading comprehension strategies while offering a variety of suggestions for helping teach readers how to use them.

Yellow Brick Roads: Shared and Guided Paths to Independent Reading 4–12
by Janet Allen
Allen takes a comprehensive look at teaching older readers through rich anecdotes from her secondary classroom; practical methods for read-aloud, shared, guided, and independent reading; and the research behind her recommendations.

Testing and Assessment

A Teacher's Guide to Standardized Reading Tests: Knowledge Is Power
by Lucy Calkins, Kate Montgomery, and Donna Santman
For the first time, teachers are challenged to consider standardized tests as a genre. Calkins and her colleagues take the mystery out of standardized testing and offer suggestions for helping students succeed on the tests.

The Case Against Standardized Testing: Raising the Scores, Ruining the Schools
by Alfie Kohn
Kohn disputes the amount of testing that students are facing in today's schools. In this book, he argues against the notion of standardized testing in an easy-to-read question-and-answer format.

Knowing Literacy: Constructive Literacy Assessment by Peter H. Johnston
Johnston creates a theoretical framework for teachers and students to thoughtfully assess literacy. Various assessment tools are profiled, such as checklists, observation forms, report cards, and portfolios.

Diversity

Other People's Children: Cultural Conflict in the Classroom by Lisa Delpit
Delpit offers her perspective on minority children in America's schools, and makes the point that academic problems among children of color are a result of the inequality within our educational system.

Reviving Ophelia: Saving the Selves of Adolescent Girls by Mary Pipher
Pipher takes a close look at the pressures on adolescent girls in our modern culture. Both educators and parents will find this book enlightening.

Savage Inequalities: Children in America's Schools by Jonathan Kozol
Kozol reveals the startling differences in America's schools by describing the state

of schooling in various parts of the country. This is a heartbreaking story that begins to explain the inequality that our students experience on a daily basis.

Reform and School Culture

Best Practice: New Standards for Teaching and Learning in America's Schools by Steven Zemelman, Harvey Daniels, and Arthur Hyde
This book features examples of standards implementation across the curriculum, subjects, and grade levels.

The Energy to Teach by Donald H. Graves
In a departure from Graves's earlier books on teaching literacy, this time he focuses on helping teachers maintain the energy they need to teach. He brings research from the business world to guide teachers in a process of figuring out how to keep alive the energy and enthusiasm that is so needed in today's classrooms.

Going Public: Priorities and Practice at the Manhattan New School by Shelley Harwayne
Going Public describes the culture at the Manhattan New School. Harwayne shares her management and leadership strategies while offering readers the opportunity to dream a little about transforming their own school.

Schools That Work: Where All Children Read and Write by Richard L. Allington and Patricia M. Cunningham
Schools That Work suggests how educators can reorganize schools to support literacy instruction by addressing issues such as resources, time, curriculum, and student assessment.

Community

Life in a Crowded Place: Making a Learning Community by Ralph Peterson
In this resource for helping teachers create a community of learners, Peterson shows teachers how to take a positive stance on classroom management to move toward more productive learning.

Brain Research

Teaching with the Brain in Mind by Eric Jensen
Eric Jensen shares the latest findings in brain research, balancing medical findings with practical classroom applications.

Useful Videos for Professional Development

Focus on Spelling by Diane Snowball
Snowball takes the viewer through authentic spelling instruction at PS 234 in Manhattan. This collection features learning words, exploring sounds, investigating letters and spelling patterns, and discovering generalizations.

Inside Reading and Writing Workshops by Joanne Hindley
The companion to *In the Company of Children,* this video series offers the rare chance to observe Hindley as she confers with students. This collection features reading mini-lessons, reading conferences, writing mini-lessons, and writing conferences.

Organizing for Literacy by Linda J. Dorn
Dorn shares ideas related to organizing the classroom for a balanced early literacy program. This collection of tapes complements her book *Apprenticeship in Literacy,* and includes organizing the classroom, learning about writing, learning about reading, and learning about words.

Strategy Instruction in Action by Stephanie Harvey and Anne Goudvis
Visit the classrooms that Stephanie Harvey and Anne Goudvis feature in their book *Strategies That Work.* Learn from these master teachers as they work with their students on reading comprehension.

Great Literature for Teacher Book Clubs

Angela's Ashes by Frank McCourt
In this Pulitzer Prize–winning memoir of his childhood in Limerick, Ireland, McCourt tells his family's story of poverty and alcoholism with a touch of Irish humor.

Animal Dreams by Barbara Kingsolver
This is the story of a woman who returns to her hometown in the Southwest to confront the issues and people she had left long ago.

The Bell Jar by Sylvia Plath
An autobiographical account, this details Plath's own mental breakdown as she fulfills a dream assignment working at a fashion magazine in New York City.

Bless Me Ultima by Rudolfo Anaya
A mystical look at how the customs of New Mexico intersect with Catholicism, this is the story of a boy and his relationship with his healer grandmother in a small New Mexican town.

The Blind Assassin by Margaret Atwood
Atwood weaves together romance, science fiction, and mystery in this Booker Prize–winning novel about a well-to-do family.

Cloudsplitter by Russell Banks
Cloudsplitter is a fictionalized account of radical abolitionist John Brown in the years preceeding the Civil War. In this tale of his actions, family life, and martyrdom, Russell Banks brings some of America's little-known history to the forefront.

The Color of Water by James McBride
This memoir tells the true story of a family with a Jewish mother, African American father, and twelve children. It was written as a tribute to McBride's remarkable, eccentric, and determined mother.

Daughter of Fortune by Isabel Allende
Allende tells the story of Eliza Sommers, the niece of a wealthy Victorian family in Valparaíso, Chile. The adventure begins when Eliza falls in love with an inappropriate young man and leaves her home to follow him to the gold fields of California.

Endurance: Shackleton's Incredible Voyage by Alfred Lansing
In this true story of Ernest Shackleton's failed expedition to Antarctica, Lansing uses sailors' logs to write this story in a narrative form. Readers feel as though they are abandoned on the ice floes alongside the crew.

Girl in Hyacinth Blue by Susan Vreeland
Vreeland begins this novel with a Vermeer painting in present day and then traces the painting backward in time and the many people it affected throughout history. The novel ends with the story of Vermeer painting the canvas.

Girl Interrupted by Susanna Kaysen
This memoir reveals Kaysen's experiences in a mental institution in Boston, sharing both its deep sadness and its morbid humor.

The Great Gatsby by F. Scott Fitzgerald
This classic novel about wealthy Jay Gatsby and his love for Daisy Buchanan takes readers to extravagant parties and quiet moments in East Hampton, New York.

High Tide in Tucson: Essays from Now or Never by Barbara Kingsolver
A book of short stories by Kingsolver, *High Tide in Tucson* delivers both Kingsolver's depth of storytelling and her scientific perspective.

The Hours by Michael Cunningham
Winner of the Pulitzer Prize, *The Hours* is a novel that blends the life and work of Virginia Woolf with Clarissa, a modern-day editor in Manhattan, and Laura, a housewife in postwar California. Together the characters converge to tell a compelling story of love and despair.

The House on Mango Street by Sandra Cisneros
Cisneros uses a poetic style in this collection of short stories featuring Hispanic characters. Humor and sadness mix in her complex storytelling.

I Know Why the Caged Bird Sings by Maya Angelou
A moving look at Maya Angelou's life, this autobiography sings the story of a talented black woman who lived a childhood of adversity, only to triumph in the end.

Jane Eyre by Charlotte Brontë
The melodramatic novel about Jane Eyre, a young girl orphaned as a child, who becomes governess to the mysterious Edward Rochester and is about to marry him when she learns a terrible secret he has been keeping from her.

Memoirs of a Geisha by Arthur Golden
Golden writes this novel using the voice of Nitta, who recounts her story of leaving her small fishing village in 1929 to become one of Japan's most famous geishas.

One Thousand White Women: The Journals of May Dodd by Jim Fergus
Using a journal format, Fergus traces the story of May Dodd, a rebellious woman from an affluent family in Boston who signs up for a U.S. government program to move to the frontier and become an Indian bride.

The Red Tent by Anita Diamant
The biblical tale of Dinah, daughter of Jacob, recounts the story of Jacob's wives, Leah, Rachel, Zilpah, and Bilhah, and how they bond with Dinah through childbirth, motherhood, and old age.

She's Come Undone by Wally Lamb
In this novel about a young girl growing into womanhood in a life devoid of love and support, Dolores finds solace in bags of potato chips and the television and fails miserably when it comes to relationships with other people.

Ship Fever by Andrea Barrett
These elegant short stories take their cue from science and the natural world as we knew it in the nineteenth century.

The Shipping News by E. Annie Proulx
Another Pulitzer Prize winner, *The Shipping News* begins with hack journalist Quoyle finding out that his wife has been killed in a car accident. Quoyle then

leaves New York to head to Newfoundland, the place of his forefathers, in this comedic and sad story of humanness.

Their Eyes Were Watching God by Zora Neale Hurston
First published in 1937, this novel by the famous writer from the Harlem Renaissance tells the story of Janie, an African American woman who doesn't have to live a bitter or sorrowful life, but instead chooses another path.

The Tortilla Curtain by T. Coraghessan Boyle
This novel has two main characters on an intersecting course of destruction. Delaney is a yuppie living in a gated community and Càndido is an illegal immigrant from Mexico squatting in the canyon nearby. As the story unfolds, their lives affect each other in ways neither man understands.

West with the Night by Beryl Markham
As revealed in her memoir of being a bush pilot in Africa in the 1930s, Beryl Markham was a daring and driven woman before her time. On the subject of *West with the Night,* Markham's friend Ernest Hemingway writes, "I wish you would get it and read it because it is really a bloody wonderful book."

Bibliography

Allen, Janet. 2000. *Yellow Brick Roads: Shared and Guided Paths to Independent Reading 4–12*. Portland, ME: Stenhouse.

Allende, Isabel. 1999. *Daughter of Fortune*. New York: HarperCollins.

Allington, Richard. 2001. *What Really Matters for Struggling Readers: Designing Research-Based Programs*. New York: Longman.

Allington, Richard L., and Patricia M. Cunningham. 2001. *Schools That Work: Where All Children Read and Write*. Needham Heights, MA: Allyn & Bacon.

———. 2002. *Classrooms That Work: They Can All Read and Write*. Needham Heights, MA: Allyn & Bacon.

Anaya, Rudolfo. 1972. *Bless Me Ultima*. New York: Warner Books.

Angelou, Maya. 1969. *I Know Why the Caged Bird Sings*. New York: Bantam.

Atwood, Margaret. 2000. *The Blind Assassin*. New York: Random House.

Banks, Russell. 1998. *Cloudsplitter*. New York: HarperCollins.

Barrett, Andrea. 1996. *Ship Fever*. New York: W. W. Norton.

Benson, Laura. 2000. "Going on Rounds: Student Work Conversations." *Colorado Reading Council Journal*. Spring 2000.

Bernard, Claude. 1997. *Quotations on Education*. Rosalie Maggio, comp. Paramus, NJ: Prentice Hall.

Boyle, T. Coraghessan. 1996. *The Tortilla Curtain*. New York: Penguin.

Boyse, J. F. 1981. *Barnes and Noble Book of Quotations*. Robert I. Fitzhenry, ed. New York: Harper and Row.

Bridges, William. 1980. *Transitions: Strategies for Coping with the Difficult, Painful, and Confusing Times in Your Life*. Reading, MA: Perseus Publishing.

Brontë, Charlotte. 1846. 2000. *Jane Eyre*. New York: Random House.

Bunting, Eve. 1994. *Smoky Night*. San Diego: Harcourt Brace.

Calkins, Lucy. 1983. *Lessons from a Child: On the Teaching and Learning of Writing*. Portsmouth, NH: Heinemann.

Calkins, Lucy, Kate Montgomery, and Donna Santman. 1998. *A Teacher's Guide to Standardized Reading Tests: Knowledge Is Power*. Portsmouth, NH: Heinemann.

Center for Collaborative Education. Boston, MA.

Cisneros, Sandra. 1991. *The House on Mango Street*. New York: Random House.

Coalition of Essential Schools. Oakland, CA.

Cunningham, Michael. 1998. *The Hours.* New York: Farrar, Straus and Giroux.

Dana, John Cotton. 1997. *Quotations on Education.* Rosalie Maggio, comp. Paramus, NJ: Prentice Hall.

Darling-Hammond, Linda. 1997. *Doing What Matters Most: Investing in Quality Teaching.* New York: Teachers College Press.

Day, Clarence. 1921. *The Crow's Nest.* New York: Knopf.

Delpit, Lisa. 1995. *Other People's Children: Cultural Conflict in the Classroom.* New York: The New Press.

Diamant, Anita. 2001. *The Red Tent.* London: Macmillan.

Dorn, Linda J. 1999. *Organizing for Literacy,* videotapes. Portland, ME: Stenhouse.

Dunn, Rita Stafford, and Kenneth Dunn. 1999. *The Complete Guide to the Learning Styles Inservice System.* Needham Heights, MA: Allyn & Bacon.

Fergus, Jim. 1999. *One Thousand White Women: The Journals of Mary Dodd.* New York: St. Martin's Griffin.

Fitzgerald, F. Scott. 1925. 2000. *The Great Gatsby.* New York: Penguin.

Fletcher, Ralph. 1993. *What a Writer Needs.* Portsmouth, NH: Heinemann.

———. 1996. *A Writer's Notebook: Unlocking the Writer Within You.* New York: Avon Books.

Fletcher, Ralph, and Joann Portalupi. 1998. *Craft Lessons: Teaching Writing K–8.* Portland, ME: Stenhouse.

Fullan, Michael. 1991. *The New Meaning of Educational Change.* New York: Teachers College Press.

Fullan, Michael, and Andy Hargreaves. 1991. *What's Worth Fighting For? Working Together for Your School.* Toronto: Ontario Public School Teachers Federation; Andover, MA: The Network, North East Laboratory; Milton Keynes, UK: Open University Press; and Melbourne: Australian Council for Educational Administration.

Golden, Arthur. 1999. *Memoirs of a Geisha.* New York: Random House.

Graves, Donald H. 1991. *Build a Literate Classroom.* Portsmouth, NH: Heinemann.

———. 2001. *The Energy to Teach.* Portsmouth, NH: Heinemann.

Guskey, Thomas, and Michael Huberman, Eds. 1995. *Professional Development in Education: New Paradigms and Practices.* New York: Teachers College Press.

Harvey, Stephanie. 1998. *Nonfiction Matters: Reading, Writing, and Research in Grades 3–8.* Portland, ME: Stenhouse.

Harvey, Stephanie, and Anne Goudvis. 2000. *Strategies That Work: Teaching Comprehension to Enhance Understanding.* Portland, ME: Stenhouse.

———. 2001. *Strategy Instruction in Action,* videotapes. Portland, ME: Stenhouse.

Harwayne, Shelley. 1999. *Going Public: Priorities and Practice at the Manhattan New School.* Portsmouth, NH: Heinemann.

———. 2000. *Lifetime Guarantees: Towards Ambitious Literacy Teaching.* Portsmouth, NH: Heinemann.

Heard, Georgia. 1989. *For the Good of the Earth and the Sun: Teaching Poetry.* Portsmouth, NH: Heinemann.

Hindley, Joanne. 1996. *In the Company of Children.* Portland, ME: Stenhouse.

———. 1998. *Inside Reading and Writing Workshops,* videotapes. Portland, ME: Stenhouse.

Honey, Peter, and A. Mumford. 1982. *Learning Styles Questionnaire: The Manual of Learning Styles.* Berkshire: Peter Honey.

Hurston, Zora Neale. 1937. *Their Eyes Were Watching God.* New York: HarperCollins.

Jensen, Eric. 1998. *Teaching with the Brain in Mind.* Alexandria, VA: ASCD.

Johnson, Spencer. 1998. *Who Moved My Cheese?* New York: Putnam.

Johnston, Peter H. 1997. *Knowing Literacy: Constructive Literacy Assessment.* Portland, ME: Stenhouse.

Kaysen, Susanna. 1999. *Girl Interrupted.* New York: Knopf.

Keene, Ellin Oliver, and Susan Zimmermann. 1997. *Mosaic of Thought: Teaching Comprehension in a Reader's Workshop.* Portsmouth, NH: Heinemann.

Kennedy, Robert F. 1981. *Barnes and Noble Book of Quotations.* Robert I. Fitzhenry, ed. New York: Harper and Row.

Kingsolver, Barbara. 1993. *Animal Dreams.* New York: HarperTrade.

———. 1996. *High Tide in Tucson: Essays from Now or Never.* New York: HarperTrade.

Kohn, Alfie. 2000. *The Case Against Standardized Testing: Raising the Scores, Ruining the Schools.* Portsmouth, NH: Heinemann.

Kozol, Jonathan. 1991. *Savage Inequalities: Children in America's Schools.* New York: HarperCollins.

Lamb, Wally. 1993. *She's Come Undone.* New York: Pocket Books.

Lambert, Linda. 1998. "How to Build Leadership Capacity." *Educational Leadership 55,* 7: 17–19.

Lansing, Alfred. 1959. *Endurance: Shackleton's Incredible Voyage.* New York: Carroll & Graff.

Little, Judith W. 1993. "Teachers' Professional Development in a Climate of Educational Reform." *Educational Evaluation and Policy Analysis* 15, 2: 129–152.

Loucks-Horsley, Susan, C. K. Harding, M. A. Arbuckle, L. B. Murray, C. Dubea, and M. K. Williams. 1987. *Continuing to Learn: A Guidebook for Teacher Development.* Andover, MA: Regional Laboratory for Educational Improvement of the Northeast and Islands.

MacDonald, Joe. 1996. *Redesigning Schools: Lessons for the 21st Century.* New York: Jossey-Bass.

Markham, Beryl. 1942. *West with the Night.* San Francisco: North Point Press.

McBride, James. 1997. *The Color of Water.* New York: Berkley Publishing.

McCourt, Frank. 1999. *Angela's Ashes: A Memoir.* New York: Simon and Schuster.

McLaughlin, Milbrey. 1990. "The Rand Change Agent Study Revisited: Macro Perspectives and Micro Realities." *Educational Researcher* 19, 9: 11–16.

Miller, Debbie. 2002. *Reading with Meaning: Teaching Comprehension in the Primary Grades.* Portland, ME: Stenhouse.

Mohr, Nancy. nd. *Peeling the Onion: Developing a Problem Protocol*. Bloomington, IN: National School Reform Faculty.

Newkirk, Thomas. 1992. *Listening In: Children Talk About Books (and Other Things)*. Portsmouth, NH: Heinemann.

Pearson, P. David, and M. C. Gallagher. 1983. "The Instruction of Reading Comprehension." *Contemporary Educational Psychology* 8: 317–344.

Pennac, Daniel. 1999. *Better than Life*. Portland, ME: Stenhouse.

Peterson, Ralph. 1992. *Life in a Crowded Place: Making a Learning Community*. Portsmouth, NH: Heinemann.

Phi Delta Kappan Research Bulletin, December 2000. No. 28.

Pipher, Mary. 1994. *Reviving Ophelia: Saving the Selves of Adolescent Girls*. New York: Ballantine Books.

Plath, Sylvia. 1971. *The Bell Jar*. New York: Harper and Row.

Proulx, E. Annie. 1993. *The Shipping News*. New York: Charles Scribner.

Rylant, Cynthia. 1985. *Every Living Thing*. New York: Simon and Schuster.

Sarason, Seymour. 1990. *The Predictable Failure of Educational Reform*. New York: Jossey-Bass.

Snowball, Diane. 2000. *Focus on Spelling,* videotapes. Portland, ME: Stenhouse.

Taberski, Sharon. 2000. *On Solid Ground: Strategies for Teaching Reading K–3*. Portsmouth, NH: Heinemann.

Tompkins, Gail E. 1994. *Teaching Writing: Balancing Process and Product*. New York: Macmillan College Publishing Company.

Tovani, Cris. 2000. *I Read It, but I Don't Get It: Comprehension Strategies for Adolescent Readers*. Portland, ME: Stenhouse.

Vreeland, Susan. 1999. *Girl in Hyacinth Blue*. New York: Penguin.

Werner, Walter. 1988. "Program Implementation and Experienced Time." *Alberta Journal of Educational Research* 34, 2: 90–108.

Zemelman, Steven, Harvey Daniels, and Arthur Hyde. 1998. *Best Practice: New Standards for Teaching and Learning in America's Schools*. Portsmouth, NH: Heinemann.

Index

Results That Last
A Literacy Model for School Change

Linda J. Dorn and Carla Soffos

2003 / 4 30-minute ½" vhs videotapes / 1-57110-362-7 / not available for rental
Produced by Ron Blome Productions

In this four-part video series, teachers and administrators explore specific ideas for implementing an apprenticeship literacy model that includes on-the-job experiences in five critical areas:

- assessing change over time in reading and writing progress;
- colleague coaching and mentoring teams in the classroom;
- school-embedded professional development;
- a curriculum that uses literacy as a means for monitoring and promoting school-wide changes;
- built-in accountability for assessing student (and program) performance.

The replicability of the model is illustrated across four schools and seven classrooms.

Tape 1: *Leadership for Literacy*
This tape illustrates the seven features of a comprehensive literacy model for school change. One of the most important features is a curriculum for literacy, which places a high priority on reading and writing and includes six essential elements of a balanced literacy program.

Tape 2: *Assessing Change Over Time in Reading Development*
The tape illustrates how teachers can use formal and informal assessments to study change in students' reading behavior, specifically changes in fluency, comprehension, and decoding abilities. It also shows how teachers can use a reading assessment wall for studying individual and group progression along a guided reading continuum.

Tape 3: *Assessing Change Over Time in Writing Development*
Here teachers will get explicit guidance and clear examples for studying change in the writing development of emergent, early, transitional, and fluent writers. An important focus is placed on the reciprocity of writing to reading, and vice versa.

Tape 4: *Teachers as Agents of Change*
This videotape provides explicit guidance for implementing coaching conferences and literacy team meetings that occur within the natural context of the school day.

The companion viewing guide provides tools for deeper exploration.

The National Board Certification Handbook
Support and Stories from Teachers and Candidates

Diane Barone, Editor
Foreword by Beverly Ann Chin

2002 / 136 pages paperback / 1-57110-349-X

Have you ever wondered what it takes to be a National Board Certified Teacher? Are you already seeking certification? Here is a practical handbook that will answer many of your questions. Beginning with the decision to seek National Board Certification, continuing through the portfolio and assessment processes, and ending with what to do if you don't successfully complete all of the requirements for certification, this book will support and guide you. Each chapter is written by a teacher or teacher educator who has been through the preparation process.

Find out:

- what National Board Certification is;
- what is expected of teachers seeking certification;
- how much time it takes;
- what the requirements are;
- what it means to be a National Board Certified Teacher.

More than a general description of the background and framework of seeking National Board Certification, *The National Board Certification Handbook* guides you through every aspect of preparing for "life during the board certification process." Contributors share examples of the student work they selected for their own portfolios, helping readers make similar decisions. Vocabulary lists, web sites, evaluation forms for video and written commentaries are also included. Interwoven throughout the book are the teachers' emotions that accompanied the process. They talk openly about their feelings so that other teachers have a sense of the emotional roller coaster that often accompanies working through this demanding certification process. From a survey to help you determine if now is the right time to seek certification, to a reminder to take vitamins, exercise, eat and sleep, this comprehensive tool can make your board certification process a little easier.

Achieving National Board Certification is a major accomplishment. It recognizes exemplary teaching that is centered on students, curriculum and the community. National Board Certified Teachers are able to demonstrate that they can teach to high standards. As a result, their students have higher achievement. If you aspire to become National Board certified or if you help teachers who are preparing for certification, this handy guide is the just-right book for you.

Visit us at www.stenhouse.com